I didn't believe
any of this

Hippie
Dippy
Bulls**t

either

I didn't believe
any of this

Hippie
Dippy
Bulls**t

either

A skeptic's awakening to
the spiritual universe

Julie Rasmussen

Red Renegade Press

I Didn't Believe Any of This Hippie Dippy Bullshit Either
A Skeptic's Awakening to the Spiritual Universe

Published by Red Renegade Press 2018, 2022
Copyright ©2018 Julie Rasmussen. All rights reserved.

Publisher's Cataloging-in-Publication data
Rasmussen, Julie Kathleen.
I didn't believe any of this hippie dippy bullshit either : a skeptic's awakening to the spiritual universe / Julie Rasmussen.
p. cm.
ISBN 978-0-692-08090-0
1. Spirituality. 2. Spiritual biography—United States. 3. Spiritual life—New Age movement. 4. Religious conversion. 5. Skepticism.
I. Rasmussen, Julie. II. Title.
BD95-131 2018
269 RAS—dc22
Author photo by Pete Toborek, badasschickphotography.com

This book is printed in the United States of America.

Correspondence may be sent to: redrenegadepress@gmail.com

Red Renegade Press

For the Warriors

"As we are liberated from our own fear, our presence automatically liberates others."

—Marianne Williamson

contents

welcome

***

introduction

Welcome to the newest edition of Hippie Dippy Bullshit! This revised edition contains more evolved descriptions of certain spiritual concepts and an updated ending that weren't present or possible in the previous edition. I hope you find these updates clear, helpful, and entertaining. -Julie

L et's get a few things out of the way before we begin.

One ... I tend to swear because "shoot, fart, and fudge" just don't get the job done.

Two ... you should know that I am an orange. Not the fruit, the color. At a leadership retreat I attended years ago, we were all given a personality test. Apparently there are four basic personalities that exist, from tribal cultures to the western world. In this test, the personalities were categorized by color:

Blues are the sensitive caregivers and the peace keepers.

Golds are the organizers and type A's.

Greens are the thinkers and problem solvers.

Oranges are all about these three-letter words: new, fun, sex.

It's not that oranges go around having fun sex with everyone new they meet, but rather, that they are gifted at making sexual innuendos out of anything.

I'm an orange.

It was an eye-opening revelation for me that I was an orange, and more importantly, that everyone else wasn't. For the first time, I realized that in all my years of cracking sexual jokes in public and assuming, *"I'm just saying what everyone else is thinking,"* that really, only one of four other people were thinking it.

So, you've been warned ... I am a potty-mouthed orange. And with that also comes the understanding that there's no subject off-limits in this book. Religion, death, beer, aliens, and Taco Bell are all on the table.

I am also a forty-something, brown-eyed, petite artificial blonde who likes cowboy boots and tattoos. I have two teenage sons. Alex, the younger, lives at home with me. I'll tell you more about him later.

I live in a small city in Colorado. My backyard is Vail, Aspen, and Red Rocks. I don't care where you live, my backyard kicks your backyard's ass. I moved us here from Denver last year and I love being out of the city. Our third-floor apartment has large windows that overlook farmland. The sticks aren't quite as rural as they used to be but compared to the city, it feels like *Green Acres* out here. The mountain views are divine and the air smells like sweet alfalfa after a rain.

It suits me perfectly.

Once I was happily settled in the sticks, I started feeling the urge to write a book.

Consider: in my adult life I had experienced a mental disorder, divorce (twice), single parenting, and swimming in the cesspool of midlife dating.

Additionally, I had also experienced becoming a successful entrepreneur, leaving organized religion, and my child coming out as transgender.

"But, damn," I thought to myself, "if I just had something to write about."

I talk to myself a lot when I drive. Sometimes I have full conversations, asking and replying to my own questions, like I'm a daytime talk show host, and my own guest, at the same time. I'll throw out some witty comment and laugh delightedly at it, savoring the perfect rapport happening between me and me.

I do this rambling all the time.

One day as I was pondering what to write about, I found myself driving around the countryside telling my life story like I was a guest speaker at a Tony Robbins retreat. My presentation was heartwarming, bringing me to tears and laughter, as I both listened and spoke. That's when I decided that I should start putting it down on paper, in my own words, how the universe took me from an insecure, judgmental perfectionist a decade ago to the open-minded, relaxed soul that I now was.

I figured I'd start writing a book of humorous, profanity-laced narrative essays explaining how my present-day peace had slowly evolved through a journey of unusual life events. That was my original plan. But as soon as I started writing, I ended up experiencing a completely unexpected, transcendental, unconditional love story of sorts, so the two got combined. You'll see what I mean.

This is my true story and its real purpose is to describe what the spiritual awakening experience (and by spiritual, I mean things pertaining to God, souls, and the universe happening outside the realm or doctrine of any religion) can feel like.

If you are spiritually curious, are on the cusp of awakening, or are already woke, this book is especially for you.

As you read, you'll see that another person was the catalyst for my awakening, which is unusual. You will also see there are some experiences described here that even I can't fully explain. But they happened. I experienced them as sure as I'm lying here in bed, typing this with Oliber (yes, with a "b" not a "v") the orange tabby, purring at my feet.

However, you absolutely get to make your own judgments on what you read. I understand that we see only what we want to see—and don't see what we *don't* want to see—so your degree of belief, or skepticism, will be entirely up to you. I suggest you brew some tea (or pour yourself a drink), relax, and allow yourself an open mind as we venture forth. It will make the ride much more fun. A few names, descriptions, and numbers were changed for privacy reasons, but all significant details remain untouched.

Go fire up the hot coals and hand me the microphone, Tony. Mama's gonna tell her own story about awakening the giant within.

## chapter one

june fucking cleaver

Nobody sets out in life to be a dick. There's an evolution to it.

I never thought I'd be a dick, partly because I always thought I was a decent enough human being, and partly because that is a term traditionally used to describe someone of the male gender. These days around my house, we don't care much about traditional gender roles, and that goes for how we use our insulting slang as well. In my book, women can be dicks and, well, this is my book.

I grew up in a two-story, forest green, middle-class home in Colorado. My dad was an alcoholic. He wasn't a mean drunk; he was an embarrassing one. I remember being six years old and physically struggling with my four older siblings to pull him inside the house, and off the front porch, where he would pass out every weekend night. My mom was usually around somewhere, but would choose to avoid the whole scene. She had given up long ago. The front porch scene was a shitty, regular routine at my house.

There's my childhood pile of crap. I assume you have one (or many) as well.

It was the '70s and there wasn't a lot of children's programming back then, so we watched old black-and-white family sitcoms like *Leave It to Beaver* after school. That's where my six-year-old mind decided that if I was just pretty and charming enough, life would be stable and full of wholesome family humor someday. If I was perfect enough, my father would surely see how lucky he was and would change his ways, solely out of love for his youngest daughter.

I just needed to be June Fucking Cleaver.

It was good in theory at six years old ... except that June Cleaver was a fictional character and attempting to re-create her in the real world was, and still is, an unobtainable, self-defeating, failure-assured goal. Not to mention that my dad's twenty-some years of alcoholism weren't something that could be fixed with an instant revelation of how "lucky" he was. Yet, that didn't stop me then or decades later from trying to be perfect.

My father's work moved us to western South Dakota when I was a teenager and I became a social butterfly—flitting around, sprinkling smart-ass wit at everything. I hated studying, so I perfected leading meaningful groups like Spanish Club instead. For me, most classes seemed pointless in the real world, except for writing and speech. I would gladly have picked up cigarette butts off the floor with my tongue at Shotgun Willie's, the local strip club, for an hour every day than sit through *any* math class. Math never made any sense to me and it still doesn't. My perfectionism shone brightest where I put most of my time and effort: in my partying skills and my hair.

I was a mild perfectionist back then, but not a dick.

I bloomed in college, mostly because the stress of home life was no longer there, and because I finally got to study what I wanted. I chose a school in southern New Mexico where I made better grades and even got my first A+ in a class, in Human Sexuality 101. I still, proudly, have that report card. The instructor had an enviable lack of modesty and always lectured unfazed by the four-foot penis projecting on the screen behind him. It was a delightful experience for this young orange.

I paid for my own schooling, so I was dirt-floor poor. I mean like Great Depression poor. I prostituted myself to the bloodmobile on campus every chance I had, donating a pint just for the free Coke and cookie afterwards. On weekends, I put on an unflattering polo shirt and worked at the mall selling tennis shoes to pay for the necessary essentials: Top Ramen, toilet paper, and cheap beer.

I studied journalism because I wanted to work in newspapers. I always loved newspapers. I thought there was something noble about being the bearer of news to the masses and the recorders of history! I spent my childhood writing dramatic front-page headlines about my stuffed animals, and I'm pretty sure I was the only nine-year-old on the block who flipped through the daily paper every evening. I loved the comics, especially *Peanuts*.

Though he was hugely popular at the time, I thought

Garfield was just fucking stupid. *Peanuts* captured the human condition with genius humor and psychological insight in its characters. Garfield hated Mondays.

That's not funny or genius.

I was a comic snob, even at nine years old.

There was a good local cartoonist in the paper that I read as well. I'll tell you more about him later, too.

I understood the fleetingness of the college years and I maxed out the experience with great appreciation. By my senior year, I could dance to the "Funky Cold Medina" at 2:00 a.m. with a full beer in each hand and not spill a single drop. I didn't walk the graduation ceremony because I didn't have the $50 for the cap and gown, so after my last test I packed up everything I owned in my 1968 Mustang and drove away.

A few years after graduation I married my college sweetheart. We were young, and we were good to each other. He was a talented golfer and was trying his hand at it professionally. We had fun, exciting adventures as a young couple driving across the country from golf tournament to golf tournament. It was the perfect postcollege experience. Eventually though, I wanted to stop traveling and settle down … and he didn't. We divorced after a few years. In hindsight, we made a perfect college couple but we were never meant to be a lifelong, adult partnership. We split the CDs, I kept the cats, and we peacefully said goodbye.

Postdivorce I settled back in Colorado. I had a growing independence going and started making new memories on my own. Unconsciously though, my perfectionism had me living a life motivated by trying to prove myself to others.

I was now a moderate perfectionist, but still not a dick.

I got married again in my late twenties. My husband was a charming, educated, handsome catch. We looked fantastic together and wanted the same things, like a stable home life and kids. I was positive that I got it right this time and we got married less than a year after we met *(note from hindsight: don't do that)*.

By our mid-thirties, we had two toddlers. We were a white, conservative, suburban family. I left any remaining cool I had at the car dealership the day I drove off in a minivan. Our Christmas card looked like an Old Navy ad and my life revolved around maintaining the illusion that nothing was ever wrong at my house. As far as anyone ever knew, our marriage was perfect, the kids were exceptional, we only bought organic, no one ever pooped, and everything was always "just fine, thanks."

Evening dinners frequently revolved around bitching about who had violated us in traffic or offended us somehow that day. If I qualified it with "They should know better than ..." or "It's just not right that ..." then somehow, I wasn't *complaining*, I was merely pointing out how the world would be better if everyone tried harder to get things right, especially when I am involved. We'd bitch for a while, then hold hands, thank God for making us better than everyone else, and pass around the organic potatoes.

Ok, now I was a dick. And a total perfectionist.

Perfectionist me took care of the kids, did the laundry, cooked, cleaned, mowed the lawn, ran the errands, paid the bills, scrapbooked every keepsake, volunteered, and made sure I never missed getting a glittery, handmade holiday card out in the mail.

It was a lot of work being June Fucking Cleaver.

I started feeling exhausted and depressingly unacknowledged from those whom I constantly sought to impress (though I don't think I could have gotten enough praise from anyone even if they tried). I was embarrassed about feeling not good enough at anything, so I started to avoid emotionally vulnerable relationships with friends, family, and my husband, lest they try to get personal and ask me how I *really* was.

I had little acceptance or compassion for myself (I was a dick to myself) and when that happened, it became impossible to have real emotional connection to anyone. I was on a slippery slope to a lonely and depressing future if something didn't change soon. Which it did, on the day that June Fucking Cleaver cracked.

Let's call it the *Leave It to Beaver* lost episode.

I was standing in line at the grocery store on an uneventful day, when suddenly I felt a terrifying sense of doom rising out of nowhere. It escalated quickly, and within a minute I was convinced that death was in the supermarket, combing the aisles, pushing a cart, and looking for me. My heart raced madly, my palms got sticky, my bottom lip trembled, and I panicked to the point that I dropped everything and frantically headed for the exit.

I was terrified and convinced I was going to pass out in the store ... which would draw a crowd ... which would end up on the news ... which would result in my children being taken away and my being put in a mental institution until I died.

It was my first panic attack. The first of about a thousand

more that were coming. That was the day my perfectionism, which I had counted on since I was six years old, stopped working and I now had panic and anxiety disorder.

I had grown into a big dick to myself and others. June Fucking Cleaver had needed to snap.

## chapter two

eat, pray, love, crack

We were cuddling, perfectly pretzel-twisted together, watching a Broncos game in bed at his place one night. I find football boring, so I was just in it for the four-hour snugs. The commentator was rambling on about strategy, timing, the defensive unit, and blah, blah, blah, blah, blah.

"He just said unit," I said.

"I know. He said penetration earlier," he replied.

Meet Bo, my twin flame and fellow orange.

What is a twin flame, you ask? A twin flame is a soulmate, a *literal soulmate*. You knew each other in the great before, and you will know each other in the great beyond. And *between* the great before and the great beyond, your paths cross in your humanness.

Now, many spiritualists believe that there are three general types of relationships in this world: karmic, soulmate, and twin flame.

Most relationships are karmic relationships. These are when two beings attract one another because intellectually, emotionally, physically, and/or spiritually you are similar. You didn't necessarily know each other in the great before, but you are on the same vibe in this life—you're on similar paths, which have converged. These can be short or long-term relationships that can take many different forms, such as romantic partners, friendships, co-workers, or acquaintances.

As far as a spiritual experience, I'd describe karmic relationships as valuable, satisfying, and frequent.

Then there's soulmate relationships.

Soulmates come with an unusual recognition that feels like you've met before (because you have). And if soulmates reconnect when *both* are near the same vibe in life (again ... intellectually, emotionally, physically, and spiritually) then meeting again feels like sublime bliss.

I'd describe soulmate relationships as knowing, harmonious, and uncommon.

Then there's twin flame relationships.

Twin flames are soulmates that reconnect when they're *not* near the same vibe in life. There's a deep soul connection pulling them together ... but there's too much human discord going on to keep them connected.

Based on my own experience, I'd describe twin flame relationships as a raging dumpster fire of unexplainable spiritual chaos and unconditional love.

Twin flame relationships are one of the most intense experiences the universe can offer in a lifetime.

And if all this sounds like complete hippie dippy bullshit to you, I hear you. That's exactly what I thought, too ... until it happened to me.

When I began to write this book in the early fall, Bo and I had just started dating again. We had originally met six months earlier, the week that I moved to the sticks. Back then, over the course of about a month, we met, had an amazing adventure together and then it all went to hell in a shitty handbasket and we broke up.

We dated other people and kept in touch after our breakup, and eventually came back together again. We had missed each other and both wanted to give it another try. It was lovely to be dating again We were getting closer, spending a lot of time together, and there were comments about the future already starting to pop up after just a few weeks. Things were looking good and I secretly started clearing out closet space for him.

I even started to envision this book being my own *Eat, Pray, Love*. Ok, maybe a little more like *Eat, Pray, Love, Crack* because my story is weirder, plus I'm an orange and I swear a lot.

I would tell the sweet, endearing story about how we met, overcame our obstacles, and finally learned to love and trust again. It would be the perfect, wrap-it-up, romantic ending! I felt giddy with excitement as I discussed the details with myself in the car.

Except that now he's gone. Again.

No more pretzel snuggling.

"I'm sorry, Julie. I just feel like I need to go," he said, as he left for the second time, after about a month again.

It broke my heart. For days, I rotated between crying, sitting in sadness, and kicking puppies. I wore dirty sweatpants and ate chips and dip in bed.

"Bu ... bu ... but there wasn't supposed to be kicking puppies in this story," I sobbed, wiping my greasy hands on my sweats, tears dripping into my French onion dip.

It was shortly after he left the second time that I came to understand that we're twin flames. I'll explain much more of those details later, but for now just know that twins separate because one or both are resisting the connection. Why? Because the soul connection is magnifying the *gap* between them and their own soul ... which feels like unsettling, inner chaos.

It's shining a light on the much needed emotional and spiritual healing to be done to reconnect their current humanness to their own soul, and thus each other. And even though he's the one that left, all that healing isn't just in his court, there's plenty of it in mine, too, as you'll see later.

Twin flame separation can last for months, years, or even lifetimes. It's hard to say. I am accepting that reality. I'm still wearing sweatpants (but I washed them) and I have taken the French onion dip off the nightstand.

So, honestly, I don't know when he'll be back. No clue. But I do know I will keep writing this book, because you and I both want to find out what happens. How will *Eat, Pray, Love, Crack* end? I guess we'll find out together.

While we're waiting, let me back up to six months ago and tell you how this whole thing began ...

* * *

"Hi, I'm looking for a Hula-Hoop instructor and I was wondering if you could help me?"

That was the first message Bo sent me through an online dating site. I had put a picture of myself Hula-Hooping in my profile and had mentioned that I was quite good at it.

I really am; I could do it for hours. I did not know this was a talent I had until I was about forty years old and my kids and I were at an outdoor summer concert in Boulder one evening. There was a vendor there selling handmade hoops. These were not like the cheap pink ones you get at the store. She made them out of heavy, bendable PVC plastic. They were big and beefy. These were the Land Rovers of Hula-Hoops.

The vendor was a cute, crunchy-looking gal wearing a long skirt and big rings. She had an area set up for anyone to come try Hula-Hooping while the music was going, so my kids pulled me over to it. I grabbed one, expecting to be terrible at it … but I was flawlessly steady, like an electric mixer. We stayed for hours.

At the end of the night, I went to an ATM to get cash and met the hippie gal in the parking lot, after dark, to buy a handmade hoop out of the back of her Subaru wagon. Only in Boulder.

Boulder, Colorado, lives up to its reputation as a mecca for progressive, intelligent, kale-eating professionals, college students, stoners, and hippies. Coloradoans know what it means to say, "Only in Boulder."

I know a story about someone buying a llama out of the back of a minivan there. Only in Boulder. Street people prefer vegan only handouts there. Only in Boulder. There are legally, no pet owners, only pet *guardians* there. Only in Boulder.

You get the picture.

So back to our dating site conversation … Bo asked me about Hula-Hoop lessons. That's cute, I thought. I checked out his profile. He looked handsome, was funny, and gave no obvious indicators of being a serial killer (my standards had sunk significantly lower over the years). We exchanged a few more messages and discovered we lived quite close to one another, so we made a quick plan to meet that night.

I met him at a local restaurant and I remember leaning around a wall and seeing him sitting there. Wow. He was a handsome ginger (not the orange-hair-freckled Howdy Doody type, but the sandier-no-freckled type) with the best jawline I'd ever seen. He was just the right amount of buff, and his blue eyes got a little squinty when he saw me, flashed me a cute smile, and gave me a friendly wave.

Damn. He was my jam.

I ordered a light appetizer because I hadn't eaten. He said he wasn't hungry, but politely told me to go ahead, though he later ate more of it than I did. That would be a future trend.

We talked about all kinds of subjects. We were equally outgoing and had the same sense of humor. It was fun and easy. Crazy fun and easy.

I noticed that he had a tattoo of a wedding band on his ring finger. I touched it, smiled, and commented, "That's an unfortunate tattoo."

He laughed and explained that as a firefighter (Yes, my twin *flame* is a *fire*fighter) he can't wear a metal ring, so he had gotten the tattoo years earlier, while he was married. He twisted it with his other hand, like there was an actual ring there, and said that the young, wise tattoo artist kept prophesying as he was working on it, saying, "I don't know, man. This is a bad idea. This is the kiss of death."

"Curse you, you man-bunned, flannel-wearing gypsy!" I said, shaking my fist in the air. We both laughed.

He'd gone to a few sessions to try and have it removed, but it was a slow and expensive process, so it was just going to remain the unfortunate tattoo.

We sat in a booth, talking and laughing for hours. We found that we were both born on Marine bases, just a few months apart, and that our dads were both named Bob.

As we walked closely together out to the parking lot at the end of the night, I realized he was probably about four inches taller than my 5'4". He was also fit and strong—very Scrappy Doo-like.

We chatted a little longer by my car, slowly inching closer to one another, with our hands in our pockets. As we reluctantly started to wrap things up to say goodbye, we both reached out for a hug and began to kiss.

We stood there, locking lips under a bright light in that parking lot for a long, long while ... making a lot of people coming out of a nearby movie theater feel terribly uncomfortable.

I honestly have no idea how long we were there. I just know we could hardly stop. It didn't feel awkward like a first kiss should.

It was incredibly satisfying.

When we finally stopped, I floated home, over the moon, on a passing cloud.

We saw each other almost every day after that. As a firefighter he'd work 48-hour shifts and then be off for four days, and since I wasn't working yet, we had a lot of time to spend together. We'd usually start by meeting for coffee in the morning. He wasn't shy and explained the poop schedule to me early on. That's when his morning coffee had processed, usually around 9:00 a.m., and he needed to poop. Eventually, we'd be at coffee and all he had to do was politely put one finger up to interrupt me during conversation, and point to his watch. Then I'd nod in understanding and make a shooing "go" hand gesture toward him.

We were almost unnaturally comfortable around each other.

We'd go for drives. We'd run errands. We'd hold hands, make jokes, and hug everywhere we went. Playful, romantic tunes would appear out of nowhere in our presence. We were a nauseating, real-life happy couple movie montage.

He had a planned vacation quickly coming up and was going to be headed to Florida, to rent a motorcycle and drive down to the Keys. As the trip got closer, what had once sounded like a great time now sounded kind of lonely to be doing alone. We talked about how we wished I was going with him, but I had just moved and wasn't even unpacked yet. I couldn't spend the money, and besides, we had just met. It wouldn't be right for me to go.

Would it?

He flew out a few days later, and two days after that, I received a random refund check in the mail from my old mortgage company for $400. No letter, no explanation, just a check. I ran it to the bank, cashed in some flight miles, and started packing. I hadn't gone on an adult-only trip for years and Mama needed a vacation badly. I made arrangements for the kids and sent him a text that said,

"Pick me up @ the Fort Lauderdale airport @ 11:00 tonight."

For four days, we rode around Florida on a Harley-Davidson. We rode to the Keys, taking in the views and soaking up sunshine. We sat on beaches, ate seafood, drank fruity cocktails, and went to a lot of Walmarts.

I'm a Westerner, I didn't realize how big Walmart is in the South. I'm in a serious, committed relationship with Target (it's actually a threesome with Taco Bell), so I felt guilty about going to Walmart, but we kept needing mundane things like sunscreen, and there were no Targets nearby. I was upfront and honest with Target about it when I got back.

It happened to be Presidents' Day weekend and it was also Valentine's Day weekend. We hadn't really thought that through and were unprepared when there were no hotel rooms available in the Keys. So, we rode back to Miami after dark … where there were also no hotel rooms.

When you're on vacation in a car, the car can be shelter for the night if needed. When you're on a motorcycle, you are screwed.

We drove around Miami until after midnight, trying every hotel we could find. We were tired, delirious, and seriously wondering what we were going to do.

We finally found the last available room in the state of Florida, at a dumpy old motel. It was one of those motels from the '50s that is shaped like a horseshoe, with a freezing cold outdoor pool and cheap plastic furniture in a middle courtyard.

The kind with vibrating beds. The owner smiled like the Joker as he ran up our almost $200 one-night bill. He gave us a key, took my driver's license as a deposit for the remote control, and showed us where our nasty room was.

We spent our first Valentine's Day together in the world's most expensive shithole.

We rode some more and went to Sarasota for a few days, where the beach sand is like soft, white baking soda. One afternoon, we stopped at a bar for a couple of Coronas and decided afterwards to take a walk along the beach.

We sauntered through the sand in our bare feet, holding hands and talking. Every so often, we'd stop to kiss, hug, stare at the water for a few minutes, and then walk some more. We walked in our sweet bliss for quite some time (and distance) kicking seaweed, picking up shells, and delightfully paying no mind to the world around us.

It was a beautiful, romantic daydream ... until we both realized we had to pee like a couple of drunk sorority girls and were now a good mile or two from the public facilities.

We were a long way from the crowds, but there were still people around so discreetly squatting in the sand wasn't an option. We were also in street clothes, so wading into the giant toilet of the Gulf of Mexico wouldn't have worked either. So, we started walking back, with our teeth now floating and the discomfort escalating quickly.

Within a few minutes, we had dropped hands. Then we stopped talking. Eventually we were both silently "wogging" with our arms swinging up high, like a couple of intense, geriatric mall walkers. A few times we tried to run, but that felt worse, so we went back and forth between little awkward sprints and the wogging. What felt like hours later, we made it back to the facilities to find lines ten-people deep for both restrooms. He was the better man and waddled into the long line to the men's room. I noticed through my tears of pain, that there was no line to the family bathroom, so I ducked in calling out, "Cody? Cody, are you in here?" and shut the door.

We spent the last night of our dream vacation in a much nicer, much less expensive hotel room than the shithole, laughing and sharing a pizza in bed. I ate one piece; he ate the rest.

As we rode the motorcycle to the airport the next day, I happily hugged him tight, resting my face on his warm back. Every few minutes, he'd smile at me in the side mirror and sweetly rub my shin or squeeze my hands, which were clasped around his middle.

As we approached the airport exit, we passed a dirty recliner dumped on the side of the road. He pointed at it and yelled back at me through the wind, "We could have slept there."

He wasn't leaving until the next day, so we said goodbye on the curb at the airport. We hugged, called each other "babe" and "hun" ... and unapologetically made out in public again. We both absoluhated to have it end. With our foreheads together, we locked eyes, said we'd see each other in a few days, then separated with grateful hearts.

I'm so thankful that every minute of that trip was a precious memory that I'll keep forever.

Because when we got back to Colorado the next week, my twin flame and I started to go to hell in that shitty handbasket.

## chapter three

shamelessly stealing napkins

I had to find a new Taco Bell recently because the one by my house seemed to be catching on that I take inappropriate amounts of napkins. I felt eyes on me the last time I was there. I take lots of napkins because you can never have enough in the car and because I use them at home for paper towels. Maybe this is clearly breaking the Mexican fast food chain/client unwritten napkin agreement, but I'm poor and lazy so I own it.

As I mentioned earlier, I am in a committed three-way with Target and Taco Bell. My sons are teenagers and let's just say we are frequent patrons. All was *bueno* until I suspected they started to notice the napkin numbers weren't adding up, so I decided maybe it was time to lay low for a while.

We tried a local competitor once, but my son Alex just sat

there staring at his paper-wrapped dinner, saying, "I can't. I feel like I'm cheating on Taco Bell."

So, we found another Taco Bell across town. We like the new one much better; it's nicer and the napkin dispenser is out of view of the front counter. When life halts you in one direction, it's to point you in a new, better one. I think that's how the universe works.

Apparently, ten years earlier, the universe had decided that June Fucking Cleaver, standing in the grocery store line, needed a new, better direction and that panic and anxiety disorder was going to get her there.

The mental thought patterns that I had used most of my life, that I was a confident, perky perfectionist with "no problems here, thanks," had exploded like a giant burrito out of a cannon that day. I now had a mental disorder telling me those patterns weren't going to work anymore, and that it was time for a new direction.

Anyone who's had a mental disorder can relate to the pain, fear, and unbearable frustration that come with it. I think that pain, fear, and unbearable frustration are purposely god-awful by intelligent design so that we are forced, out of misery, to redirect ourselves in new and better directions.

God made sure god-awful was as bad as it gets ... but for the right reasons.

My anxiety was god-awful. She was a mean, repetitive bitch and I hated her. In the beginning, she controlled every part of my day; I avoided driving in heavy traffic and being in stores because I feared panic attacks and the whole "*and I'll be put in a mental institution until I die*" scenario.

When I wasn't having full-on panic attacks, my anxiety would get cruelly obsessed on some irrational thought that would have me constantly stressed out.

I used to picture my obsessive thinking looking like the Heisman Trophy statue. You know, that statue of a college football player clutching a football under one arm and protecting it with his other outstretched arm.

My mind would grab a hold of some strange, obsessive thought, usually an irrational health fear like, "*I'm sure I've got some rare flesh-eating disease*," and clutch it tightly.

Then, thrusting the other arm out to protect the absurd fear, my mind would charge down the field, dodging tackles to get that stupid thought into the end zone.

But it wouldn't stop there. It would continue compulsively on … plowing through the band, down the tunnel, and out the stadium ala Forrest Gump. It would just keep running—over the hills, into the distance, clutching that doomsday thought all day and night with no purpose.

It only stopped when I encountered a new, usually worse, irrational fear that my mind would then obsessively clutch. All it took was watching a *60 Minutes* story on bird flu, for example, to put me back on the 10-yard line again, repeating the same miserable, pointless process.

I decided that I would go to my regular doctor first, to see if medication would at least help control the symptoms of the attacks. I was having one or two attacks every day. During a panic attack, the mind floats away from reality into a hazy fear level that is way beyond normal, especially given the circumstances (e.g. standing in line at the grocery store). With that psychological fear comes physical symptoms ... a racing heart, trembling, and the feeling of fainting coming on.

The doctor gave me a prescription and I took one pill. That's all. One pill. I truly hated how the medication made me feel. It didn't just take away the anxiety, it took away *all* of my emotions. I felt like a zombie housewife.

I also worried that if I was on meds, would I ever really know if I was getting better? And what would happen when I stopped them? I weighed my options and reluctantly decided that I would do this the slow, painful, m*%$er f&@#ing, s*#-of-a-b%#ch! hard way ... I'd retrain my thinking, without drugs, to get over this.

I started with regular therapy. The therapist I tried wanted to talk about my childhood, which at the time I thought was stupid, plus I really hated that she wore Crocs so I quit after one visit.

Next, I tried hypnotherapy. Hypnotherapy is a fascinating thing. It's a different, more direct route to getting to the root of problems, which is how impatient me liked things. Maybe it's not for everyone, but I will say it worked well for me. While hypnotized, the therapist asked me to go to the origins of my anxiety.

I saw a movie running in my mind and it was as if I was watching from next to the projector.

The scene was a bedroom in my '70s childhood home. It was also my mom's sewing room (moms used to sew). The walls were a golden yellow and the bedding was rust colored. There were bookshelves full of folded fabric and kids' things lining the walls. I saw my six-year-old self sitting on brown carpet, playing with records. I had a collection of Disney movie records with big read-along picture books attached. You couldn't rent or buy movies back then, so those records were the only way to experience *The Aristocats* or *101 Dalmatians* again until they came back to theaters. God, I loved listening to those records. They were a happy peace in my not-so-happy home.

I had expected to see some vision of my drunk father appear as the movie played, but it didn't happen. What I saw instead was a sad scene of me desperately wanting attention from my mother, with her back to me, focused on her sewing machine. I felt the pain of the moment and I wept as I watched. It wasn't just my father's alcoholism; I was the youngest in a big family and had felt emotionally ignored by my mother.

Clearly, I had more childhood piles of crap than I thought. That damn therapist and her Crocs were right, it all *does* go back to childhood.

I decided to continue with self-therapy after that, so I went to the bookstore to find some workbooks. Do you know how comforting it was to find that there's a *Panic Attacks for Dummies* book? It was a much-needed confirmation for me that this problem was mainstream, and that I was not alone. I found some books that worked well for me, and as the months went by I came to realize that the origin of my anxiety was lifelong shame. I had taken on shame from my father's drinking. I had taken on shame from feeling unworthy of love and attention.

That constant cloud of shame was all that I knew. I had been trying to overcompensate for my shame by being perfect since I was six years old.

In the years of self-therapy that followed, I opened up my past and looked at it again, as an adult. I learned that as young children we aren't developed enough to process dysfunction in an effective way, so instead we cope in the moment. Those coping mechanisms that protect us in childhood, like becoming a perfectionist to cover up shame, can stick with us into adulthood, where they can be destructive little bastards, attacking our ability to form healthy self-esteem and emotional intimacy with others.

The more I read, journaled, and talked to myself in the car, the more I was able to reconcile some peace with my childhood circumstances—acknowledging and accepting that they were out of my control. I saw that shame never was my burden to bear. And when the shame cloud finally began to lift, so did the anxiety. It has not been back since.

I did it without drugs. I did it the m*%$er f&@#ing, s*#-of-a-b%#ch! hard way. And in doing so, I opened my eyes to the reality that I was a warrior and a mental beast.

At the time, I looked at panic and anxiety disorder as a suffering that I had to overcome. Now though, I look back at it differently. The suffering wasn't my enemy. The suffering is what, thankfully, kept me working harder every day for a new direction and a better life. The emotional discomfort is what made me keep doing the work to replace my old, perfectionist thought patterns with new, healthier ones.

The suffering kept reminding me of how I *didn't* want to live. It was a loving friend that wouldn't relent until I turned my thoughts in a new direction.

The healing that happened as a result of my anxiety was, thankfully, the peaceful demise of sweet June Fucking Cleaver.

And the birth of a bold and unapologetic napkin thief.

## chapter four

heaven, hell, and which has better donuts

We're very spoiled where we live. We have the Rocky Mountains and the Great Plains available to entertain us, depending on our mood. Alex and I like to go for drives, and a drive to Wyoming is when we're in the mood for wide open spaces. Cheyenne is north of us, right over the state line, so we go there for donuts. Not cool gourmet donuts, just boring grocery store donuts.

You know, the round ones.

We'll get our donuts and cruise through the old brick downtown to see what's going on. Cheyenne is one of the best Old West towns in the country; it's full of cowboy charm. My grandparents lived in Cheyenne for fifty-some years, and it's always been my home away from home. If a city can be a warm blanket out of the dryer, Cheyenne is it for me.

I grew up going to Frontier Days there every July. My siblings and I would dress up like cowboys (ok, we put on bandanas) and get in a huge, snaking line downtown for the free pancake breakfast. There would be lots of activities going on—banjos twanging away, couples square dancing, and volunteers flipping pancakes all around us. It smelled like coffee, ham, and maple syrup for miles.

As a kid, it was a big, sticky heaven.

We'd stay for hours, eating, watching the airshow, and wandering the midway of carnival rides.

We never did go to the rodeo. In fact, in all the years I've lived in the West, I've never been to a rodeo. I can't use, with any real honesty, the phrase, "This isn't my first rodeo."

At the end of the day, we'd meet up with my cousins at my grandparents' nice townhome and eat takeout fried chicken. You know, them big-ol'-buckets with mashed taters, too. Because we had a big family we rarely ate out, so it was the greasiest, tastiest meal of the entire summer. I gleefully licked every Styrofoam gravy container clean.

My brilliant grandmother taught me everything I need to know about entertaining: put on an apron, pour yourself a scotch and water, and let someone else do the cooking. She was a petite woman with perfectly coiffed hair and great style, and she always smelled like expensive English lavender soap. She was the educated and social doctor's wife in town, and I never saw her make a single thing from scratch. Therefore, neither shall I.

These days my grandparents and their townhome are long gone, so Alex and I get our donuts and stop in at a good comic book store downtown, where the owner, a friendly young guy with a freakishly good memory, remembers us every time. We usually wander around for a while, Alex buys a comic book, and then we head back to the car.

On the way back to Colorado there's a billboard that we pass with clouds and flames on it, that says in huge letters something like:

"IF YOU CROAK TONIGHT … HEAVEN OR HELL?"

Alex and I always read it out loud and shout out our responses …

"If I croak tonight, I'm going to Taco Bell!" I yell.

"And I'm going to a gay bar!" he adds with enthusiasm, pumping both fists into the air.

I respect and appreciate that we have the freedom to express our beliefs in this great country, but I'm not a fan of that billboard for two reasons:

First, I don't like *any* advertising that uses fear tactics.

Second, I don't like the font. It's very blocky.

I started attending big, non-denominational Christian churches in my late twenties when I met my second husband. We had both grown up in traditional (boring) churches, so these come-in-your-flip-flops places were an exciting change. They were full of nice people with whom we had a lot in common. Socially it was great, the music was modern, the sermons were funny and relevant, and they had flavored creamers at the coffee table.

We loved it and dove in head first.

Eventually our faith became serious business in our marriage. We'd pray in restaurants, send super Jesus-y Christmas cards every year (it wasn't that I was anti-Santa, I was just pro-Jesus during those years), and we loved to tell friends and family that "we'd pray for them" whether they wanted it or not.

As much as I now see that I was incredibly annoying about it, my intentions were good, and I really did believe in God. I was deep into my faith when I went through panic and anxiety disorder, and it definitely helped me get through it the m*%$er f&@#ing, s*#-of-a-b%#ch! hard way. I turned to a higher power for support a lot during the worst of those times.

My husband and I proudly called our faith "the rock that would always hold us together," and it might have, except that it didn't equip us with the self-esteem and emotional intimacy skills that we both lacked.

Admittedly, our relationship had sort of morphed into a practical partnership over the years, but I assumed we were both committed enough to the *blah* to keep it going. Apparently, however, we weren't in agreement on that, and I was not prepared when divorce came about, after thirteen years, with little warning. I would have to get perspective and deal with feelings later. First, I was going to have to comfort my kids, find a new place to live, go back to work (which I hadn't done in ten years), and a hundred other things that I was not prepared for.

I'd been through god-awful before. I could handle this.

I needed a job. I had done a lot of home improvement over the years, flipping and staging some houses, so I went to work at Home Depot and I loved it. It was a simple, no-brainer position where I pretty much got paid to socialize. What I loved the most there was the variety of people that I worked with, a lot of them in transition, like me. There were retirees still working to pay the bills, empty nesters, single parents, and college students ... all there, doing life. Yes it's cheesy, but they were a big, happy family to me at a time when that was exactly what I needed.

I loved that place, and the smell of lumber will always make me sentimental.

The other thing I loved about it was the ridiculous amount of sexual innuendos.

If you've ever felt surprisingly frisky after leaving the home improvement store, here's why: In there, you're surrounded by caulk (listen to it), screws, lubricants, ropes, chains, tie-downs, bent shafts, straight shafts, ballcock nuts (yes, it's a real thing), and nipples. And if you're lucky, a cashier will offer to "check you out and get you loaded."

I was not the only employee who noticed this. All the other oranges knew it, too, and yes, we'd snicker behind your back when you'd ask what aisle the stripper was in.

So, I had a job. Next, I found a nice little brick ranch to buy and I moved the kids and myself in. We set up a parenting agreement where they saw their dad on weekends. I smiled and waved them off every Friday night, then drove around for hours, crying and talking to myself in the car.

I kept going to church during and after my divorce. It was a comforting stability amid the complete uncertainty that was now the rest of my life. I called it my "shelter from the storm" back then. I was grateful for the sermons that always seemed perfectly timed and eerily directed at me.

But after some time, my motivation to go shake hands and

sing along began to wane. I started to feel flat about it. Maybe because going reminded me too much of a past that I was now moving on from, but also because my growing independence and confidence were calling me to start questioning some of the holes in my religion that had always secretly bothered me.

As much as there were meaningful, comforting things about it, there were also things that I struggled with.

I no longer wanted to ignore that I'd been practicing shopping cart religion. That's where I'd go along and take "this bit" of doctrine off the shelf and put it in my cart because I believed it, but would then quietly leave something else next to it on the shelf because "*that really doesn't make sense in today's world*" or "*that's not all that important.*"

I began to think that a relationship with a perfect deity shouldn't have any reasons for shopping cart religion to even exist.

The subject of homosexuality was becoming the biggest shopping cart problem for me. At my new job, I had made some wonderful friends, a few who happened to be gay. It was the first time that homosexuality had become personal to me. I really loved these people. They were funny, successful, good-hearted friends, most of them in committed relationships. The subject was now in my backyard, as I like to say, and I felt conflicted.

Living in South Dakota in the '80s, homosexuality was not a subject that got discussed. As good Midwesterners, we, for the most part, politely pretended not to see or talk about it.

Later as an adult, I didn't think of homosexuality as a choice that someone makes, but I never defended it as natural either. I just continued to politely avoid the subject. The churches I attended essentially did the same thing. There was an unofficial understanding that homosexuality was to be considered a life-style choice until further notice, and that it was best to never bring it up.

But when pushed to really examine the subject for the first time in my life, my logic told me nobody chooses to be gay any more than one chooses to be straight. I do not recall any moment in my life that I made a conscious decision to be straight. I just was.

In my mind, I finally decided that people are born straight, and people are born gay.

So why then, would a truly loving creator create someone as naturally gay but then judge that as sin?

The logic wasn't there.

And yes, I am big on logic. I always have been. If I was on *Star Trek*, I'd be Spock. It would be the only logical choice.

I took the Mensa test a few years ago and passed. Mensa is a worldwide snob society for people with high I.Q.s. Passing the Mensa test means I score in the top 2% of the population on an I.Q. test. It really means that my aptitude for logic, reasoning, and problem solving is very high. I'd like to brag and take all kinds of credit for my high score, but it's not something I stud-ied for. I just came pre-packaged with it at birth.

Having a high I.Q. also doesn't mean I'll win on *Jeopardy*, because high aptitude can be present in some brain functions but not others. For instance, I could confidently discuss the depths of the human psyche with Freud over coffee ... but I couldn't do the math to tip the waitress when we were done.

Passing the Mensa test was a weird validation for me. I have always had big, crazy, hairbrained ideas (like "Hey, I could write a book!"), but most of my life I felt foolish about them. This was mostly because growing up, my home life and school life weren't exactly places that embraced hairbrained ideas. So I assumed, and was even told at times, that I was a flighty dreamer.

I ended up taking the Mensa test because Alex was testing as academically gifted in school. I was baffled as to how that was possible given that both his dad and I were solid C students, so I took a practice I.Q. test out of curiosity.

I was disappointed with my first effort, but later realized I had actually done quite well ... I had just added my score wrong.

I scored high enough on the practice test to give the $40 Mensa test a try. Plus, I thought it would help my résumé if I passed, which surprisingly, I did.

I include all of this in my story to:

1. Give some credibility to my statements about logic.

2. Tell all the current or former C students with hairbrained ideas out there that grades are not indicators of potential. School is mostly about test-taking skills and memorization. *Life* is about logic, reason, risk taking, and so much more. Dream big, my flighty friends! Your crazy is genius and the A students will probably work for you one day!

So, my Mensa-level logic was struggling with why a truly loving God would create people as naturally homosexual, but then judge that as sin.

I decided it was time to follow my expanding spiritual curiosity because either my understanding of homosexuality was wrong or maybe my understanding of God was wrong.

I felt guilty about questioning my old beliefs, but I could expand my views without completely abandoning them.

And I figured God is big enough to allow, and even encourage, logical questions.

I envisioned God kindly and calmly saying, "I'll bring the coffee, you bring the donuts, and we'll chat."

## chapter five

# of sweater vests and star wars

He switched his drink over to his prosthetic hand and shook mine with his other. "Hi, I'm Aaron," he said, shining a toothy smile at me, as we were both gathered at the punch table. He was the outgoing, friendly sort, like I had become again since my divorce. He was in his mid-forties, medium height, with a head of slightly thinning brown hair, an athletic build, and a seriously great smile.

We were at an open house for a mutual friend's business and it was just a few weeks after I had started to expand my spiritual curiosity. I introduced myself, we made some small talk, and after a while the subject of his prosthetic arm came up. He told me that he had been in a motorcycle accident a few years prior and that he shouldn't even be alive. He pointed like a tour guide to all the titanium limbs that he now had. He also told me that he had a near-death experience during the accident. My eyebrows shot up and I eagerly leaned in asking for details, which he was glad to provide.

"I saw some loved ones that had passed and Jesus standing there, greeting me," Aaron described. He then went on to explain how he also felt an enormous presence of love, light, and peace. He said his experience ended when he saw Jesus holding the hands of his two children (who are living) and him being told, "It's not your time; you're going back for your kids."

Which he did.

Aaron smiled big when he was done and said, "I'm relieved I saw my maker. I must be doing something right."

Aaron is doing it right. He's part of a non-profit that restores bicycles for kids. He's an avid cyclist himself, a loving father, and a straight-up good guy.

I'm glad Jesus sent him back.

In the weeks following our conversation, I kept thinking about Aaron's experience. I had read stories about near-death experiences, and most Christians describe the same thing … being greeted by Jesus and a huge presence of light, love, and peace that made them not want to come back to Earth. I began to wonder though, what do people of other faiths and cultures describe in their near-death experiences?

In a quick internet search, I found that generally the figure who greets you with the pen and clipboard, i.e., Jesus, can vary from faith and culture, but the consistency is that enormous, loving, peaceful presence.

"*Is that peaceful presence God?*" I asked myself. "*And if so, if we take away religion, are we all worshipping the same God?"*

It was the first time that I had ever considered God outside of religion. I started contemplating God as being, not a Gandalf-looking, bearded-guy-in-the-sky figure, but rather a loving, spiritual presence, like what Aaron had described.

A presence, maybe ... more like ... well ... The Force in *Star Wars*.

Now the word "spirituality" had always given me pictures in my mind of overly dramatic art, the kind you see at outdoor summer craft shows, of some oily, naked couple with wings reaching for the moon. But spirituality was the word I kept gravitating to as my thoughts on God and faith evolved over the following months.

I wondered what the difference between religion and spirituality was, so I asked Google one day and got this general summary (in my own words): Religion is accepting and adhering to a set of beliefs. Those beliefs are learned thoughts. Spirituality is awareness and connection to our divine higher consciousness.

"Ok, what is our divine higher consciousness?" I asked next.

I got 22,000,000 results that time (Geezus, was I living under a rock to not know what divine higher consciousness was?). As I scrolled through links and articles on the subject, I stopped at the name Eckhart Tolle, a German-born, worldwide best-selling author and speaker. I clicked on a YouTube link of one of his talks, which I watched, then another, and another. I kept this up for the next few hours.

He looked like a middle-aged college professor. He had a round face, a full head of light brown hair, and in most of the videos he was wearing a neatly pressed, button-up shirt and a comfy sweater vest.

There were no oily, winged, naked couples in sight.

As I watched his videos, in a soft German accent, he spoke so logically about our divine higher consciousness. There was no shopping cart religion in what he was saying because he wasn't talking about religion. What he was talking about really seemed to be a cross between psychology, philosophy, and spirituality. What he was saying made sense to me; it was just plain logical. I'd say that over the next few months, I became a regular student of his and other mainstream spiritual teachers like Deepak Chopra and the late Wayne Dyer.

And that's what they were, teachers. Not men to be worshipped, just teachers.

Our divine higher consciousness is essentially what I would call my soul, I decided after some time. I could also call it my inner being, my higher self, or my true self. There's no universal rule book on what to call it. It's the divine part of me that always remains in the non-physical world. My personality is a human extension of my soul. And my body is the vehicle for that extension.

In a television interview, *The New York Times* #1 best-selling author of the *Seat of the Soul*, Gary Zukav, once described our personalities as small boats and our soul as our mothership, always there and guiding us safely ... if we chose to follow.

I like his ship analogy, and I add my own twist to it.

The mothership is part of the *fleet* that is God/the Universe/ Steve. My soul is part of the *insanely* efficient crew that makes up the mothership and I am the small boat following that mothership. The mothership and crew never get lost or lose me, I just drift away from them at times.

Our soul is also what we find when we separate ourselves from our egos.

Basically, the common message of all the spiritual teachers that I followed was that our ego and our soul are two different voices always going on in our head. Our ego is the fear-based, usually shitty, human voice that thrives on constantly feeding us negative messages like, "You should be worried because the whole world is happier, braver, kinder, smarter, thinner, richer, more responsible, more popular, more lovable, better-smelling, and better-looking than you."

Your ego is not your amigo.

Deepak Chopra perfectly calls our egos, "a socially induced hallucination." It's the thought-generating entity in us that we tend to think is who we *are*, but it's not. Our *souls* are who we are. We just have a hard time connecting to and living like our souls, because our blabbering egos never shut up.

I see our egos as having a mental net attached to them, always trapping fear-based feelings and labels for ourselves—labels that we acquire as we relate to other ego-identified people (i.e., society) throughout our lifetime. Over time, that net becomes full of irrational fear, insecurity, and victim mentality from the dysfunction that we've experienced, which the ego then loves to, dutifully, pull out of the net and regurgitate to us constantly.

It especially likes to gather all our negative experiences and tell us that the sad stories of our lives are who we are, and that we are doomed to repeat them.

Thus, most of us completely waste the present, worrying about the future, based on experiences of the past.

What I began to understand as I studied a variety of spiritual teachers, is that when we *recognize* our ego doing its thing, and become an observer to it, it loses its power over us. Diffusing that power then allows us to make that greater connection to our soul ... where infinite clarity, intelligence, and love abide.

I loved hearing that my ego was not who I am! To see that my past problems were not who I was, but rather, that they were just experiences in my life, was freeing. I didn't need to identify myself by them anymore. They aren't who I am.

My soul is who I *really* am.

I think one of my favorite things I learned at that time through those teachings was that we don't need to "learn to love ourselves."

We *are* love. We just need to learn to stop listening to our egos.

That made so much sense to me. I'd always found the idea that I needed to "learn to love myself" a statement that is difficult to practice in reality. Now I could see why. Our egos won't *let* us love ourselves.

I heard it explained well in the form of a Cherokee story about two wolves: One evening an old Cherokee Indian told his grandson about a battle that goes on inside all people.

He said, "My son, the battle is between two wolves inside us all. One is anger, jealousy, regret, guilt, and ego. The other is joy, peace, kindness, truth, and love."

The grandson thought about it for a minute and then asked his grandfather, "Which wolf wins?"

The old Cherokee simply replied, "The one that you feed."

The love for myself that I was looking for didn't need to be added to my life, it was already there. All I really needed to do was stop feeding my ego.

I now had a new awareness of these two voices, and over the next few years, the more I practiced recognizing my ego in action, the easier it got. I could observe when my ego was needlessly probing me to be defensive or resentful. I also began to see that most things I'd ever feel slighted over were never intended as personal attacks at me, yet my ego would waste all kinds of time working up ways to criticize others, defend myself, and blame, blame, blame ... when instead, I could have just been shrugging my shoulders and moving on.

It was an extremely liberating revelation.

At the same time, the more I connected to my loving soul, the kinder and more compassionate I became. The biggest difference by far was my expanding acceptance of others, which had already started with my changing views on homosexuality. The more I quit identifying with my ego (that was always judging me so negatively), the more I quit judging others.

In the past, I had been great at loving others like me, but I was self-righteous toward those who didn't believe what I believed. With good, protective intentions my ego simply had me believing that I was right about my understanding of God, sin, and the Universe, and that those who believed anything else were wrong. I was embarrassed to now look back and see how I had failed to respect the beliefs of billions of other human beings.

As I kept moving toward simple, soul-based spirituality and away from religion, I thought a lot about the reality of God and Jesus and how they connected into all this souls and ego business. I still absolutely believed that there is an infinite, intelligent, eternal "Source" constantly at work. Call it The Force, call it God, call it the Universe, call it Steve. The name doesn't matter.

In fact, in Taoism (pronounced dow-ism) that Source is called the Tao, and Taoists believe that the Tao that *can* be named is not the eternal Tao. *It's just so infinite and powerful* that trying to put a human label on it is impossible.

The name doesn't matter, because they're all too limiting. Call it what you please. God/the Universe/Steve knows what you're talking about.

I also still believed that Jesus was real. But I started to think that maybe it's possible, that somewhere over thousands of years of translations, interpretations, and egoic agendas, we humans ... err ... buggered up his story.

My perspective on who he was was starting to change.

"Was Jesus fully aware of the two voices in our head?" I started to wonder. Was he a *man*, a spiritual teacher, who had transcended his ego and was thus living in pure alignment with his own soul? Was his purpose to actually teach that *any* man can achieve that alignment himself?

Did our egos lead us outside of ourselves, to start worshipping the teacher, instead of just following his teachings? Are we misinterpreting what his real message was?

It wasn't crazy to consider.

I could see why I had never questioned such things before, because I had always been *unaware* there was a fear-based ego in my head telling me not to.

It was becoming clearer to me, that despite what I had grown up believing, there's more than one path to God. All the great spiritual teachers and teachings were mine to freely question, combine, and study in search of my own truth.

I never would have dreamed that I would become closer to God and more Christ-like *after* I left the church, but that's exactly what happened.

## chapter six

the shitty handbasket

Before I had even washed my dirty laundry from our Florida trip, things started to feel different. Like a bee, I sensed fear.

Sadly, I could feel Bo was pulling away. Over the next couple of weeks, he kept making a point to interject in our conversations, "We're just too different; this can never work."

He would hint at breaking up ... and then we were fine ... and then at breaking up ... and then we were fine. I was growing tired of his waffling. I told him to make up his mind if he was "in" or "out" of this relationship. So, in a painful, lousy conversation about it one night, he finally told me that he was "out."

I told him, very ladylike to "go to hell," and then I slammed the front door so hard on my way out that the hinges probably fell off.

As I drove home, I realized that I had never felt so sad and disappointed over a relationship ending.

I was really going to miss him.

Did he not feel what I felt? What just happened?

Whenever he was waffling, he kept clinging to that statement, "We're just too different; this can never work."

And we were. I won't disagree.

He was raised that you go to church, believe in the Gandalf God, and that homosexuality is wrong.

I didn't go to church, I saw God as The Force from *Star Wars*, and I was the new queen of the Pride Parade.

So yes, we had some differences. We knew this about each other from our second date. I acknowledged that our view of God was different, but that it was still the same idea of a loving, eternal, omniscient presence. I had also told him that I was an ally of the LGBTQ (Lesbian, Gay, Bisexual, Transgender, Queer) community because as far as I was concerned, love is love, and someone's anatomy or gender as it pertains to that is simply none of my business.

I honestly didn't put much weight into our differences because when ever we did discuss those subjects, he never seemed the slightest bit insensitive or homophobic to me. I sensed that he felt he should defend his religious beliefs, but it didn't seem to me like he completely believed them.

But I also understood that he'd been taught since childhood that he shouldn't partner with, or trust others, who don't share his same beliefs.

I had compassion for him that the idea of questioning his lifelong spiritual principles came with the fear in his mind of realistically, well … *going to hell*.

I could see why our differences were difficult for him.

The snow was melting. Winter had started to turn into spring, and though it had been a few months since the door-slamming breakup night, I was still trying to make peace with our relationships ending.

I wanted to move on, but I just wasn't.

I decided it must be because we didn't have a healthy closure to things. I had matured enough to know that healthy closure is a good thing (and it didn't take Dr. Phil to see that the clanging of hinges falling off a slammed door was not exactly healthy), so I decided to stop in one day at the gym he goes to, to see if I could catch him, and hopefully, make amends.

He was there and greeted me with a warm smile and those blue, squinty eyes, which I was happy to see. We headed out to the parking lot, where he opened the tailgate of his pickup truck for us to sit down. He looked good and the comfortable ease between us, that had started on our first date, was still there. He seemed glad to see me and eager to talk as well. As we both settled down on the metal of the tailgate, I told him that I hoped we could make peace, because apparently I was having a hard time moving on without it.

As we sat next to one another, mostly looking down at our dangling feet, I told him that he was special to me and that our breakup had hurt me badly.

He acknowledged my words with apologetic nods as he listened.

"What happened?" I asked with sincerity.

He turned to face me, and told me that I was special to him, too.

He told me that although he cared deeply about me, I also came with beliefs that were totally different from all he had ever considered. He said that he left because, with our differences, he felt that we couldn't ever truly be what the other wanted.

He frowned and said he wished he didn't feel that way, and that it hurt him as well.

"I'm really sorry," he said, holding my hands in his.

We both agreed that we were glad for the talk. I apologized to him as well, for how I had reacted to our breakup that night. I was hurting and my words were harsh.

I asked if he replaced the hinges.

We accepted each other's apologies, stood up, and tightly and silently embraced for a long, long while.

Then we said goodbye and walked our separate directions.

He's not wrong, I thought to myself, as I got into my car.

I couldn't go back to sharing his beliefs ... and I suppose he didn't think he could ever share mine.

How very sad.

"Move on," I told myself as I sighed heavily, wiped a few tears, and drove away.

* * *

As summer approached, I decided to try online dating again. It had now been several months since our breakup, and I figured moving on and getting back out there was what I needed next.

I am in that weird generation of old-people online daters. It makes my kids go "ewww." Millennials will never know life without online dating, but we Gen-Xers had to learn online suitor shopping midlife, and I think we deserve some kudos for that.

I remember when I was first contemplating dating after my divorce. As many people do during that time, I was questioning how dateable I was. The last time I was single I was in my twenties, and now here I was in my forties, and I really had no clue at all what I looked like to the rest of the dating world. Was I hot? Was I old? Was I Momish?

I was thinking about that as I walked down a sidewalk in Boulder with Alex around that time. For reasons I don't recall, I was wearing a dress shirt, a tight-fitting skirt, and heels. As we walked along, a carload of University of Colorado guys drove past, whooped it up, and yelled at me, "You're a certified MILF!" *(MILF, if you're not an orange, is a term from the movie* American Pie. *It's code for a hot mom ... a mom I'd like to fuck.)* Yes, it was crass and foul but I had to laugh (and appreciate the clarity—apparently I was hot *and* momish). It was a decent enough nudge to get me back out there.

The whole online dating thing is such a strangely ridiculous blessing and curse. There are things to hate about it, like how it makes dating disposable and lends itself to rudeness. In real life, we generally don't abruptly walk away from someone mid-conversation because that would be incredibly awkward, but it happens frequently in online dating conversations.

The blessing of online dating is that it's an easy way to meet compatible people quickly.

This is Colorado, so 50% of male profiles are a guy hiking a fourteener (a 14,000-foot mountain) with his dog, followed by a description of how he is "really different than most guys" in that he likes hiking, live music, sports, and yada, yada, yada.

I had probably been on thirty-some dates over the years since my divorce, and I will honestly say, not one of them was terrible. Most of the men I met were good guys.

A few were unusual though.

Like the sweet and cute, secret heavy drug user.

This was our third date ...

Him: Do you ever smoke pot?

Me: You mean the Devil's lettuce? No. I have no strong opinion on it though. Do you smoke?

Yes.

A lot?

Kind of.

"Kind of" like a few times a month? Or a few times a week?

More like a few times a day.

Oh. (long pause)

Do you ever do hard drugs?

Damn, dude. I can see where this is going.

Then there was the guy who had the same mannerisms and facial features as one of my nieces. It didn't matter that he was twenty-plus years older than she, *and a man*; I kept sensing all these creepy similarities between them. Hells no was that going anywhere. Talk about "ewww."

And then there was the kinky sex guy. He was an intelligent, nice, white collar professional and he was upfront in his profile that he likes kinky sex. I told him that I had never thought about that and wasn't sure that it would work for me, but since we really did get along well, why not meet for sushi one night. We had quite a bit of time to chat before a table was available, so we sat outside and had a nice time talking about business ideas and other random things.

As soon as we sat down though, he told me that kinky sex was a "requirement" for him in a relationship.

I wasn't ready to commit to that.

I hadn't even finished my miso soup yet.

Dating helped occupy my mind for a few months, but I was still thinking about Bo most every day. I missed our talks, the poop schedule, and the sweet Southern way he called me "ma'am." I missed the cute way he'd tilt his head back when he'd laugh. I missed his presence in my life.

Though he and I had agreed to give each other space, we would randomly text some dumb meme as an excuse to say "hi" every few weeks as the months went on. We even met for an afternoon beer a couple times to see if we could be friends. Being friends never really worked, because there was always an energy between us that felt like more.

One time, over a beer, he told me had been doing some soul searching and would now admit to me that he actually *did* want us to work so badly.

"But our beliefs are just too different, Julie," he said.

To which I responded by grabbing the closest steak knife and gouging it in his eye socket.

After a few "let's be friends" afternoon beers (that always ended in heavy sighs and big hugs as we parted), I started to realize that we didn't ever truly let each other go. There was some magnet that kept pulling us back, despite our best efforts to leave each other for good. So really, why weren't we just *being* together?

True, we really *didn't* make sense. But at the same time, we talked like best friends, had the same sense of humor, cared deeply about each other, and were stupidly attracted to one another.

This was confusing.

Were our differences really enough to keep us apart?

## chapter seven

differences schmifferences

I shuffled my filthy pink, fuzzy slippers into the kitchen and headed toward my unsophisticated coffee maker. I could hear my son Alex making clunking noises in his bathroom. As I leveled off a scoop of grounds and shooed Oliber (and his fresh-from-the-litter-box paws) off the counter, Alex came into the room walking tall and delicately, like a young giraffe. He was wearing a silver sequin dress, drag queen makeup, and a red wig with bangs that reminded me of Wynonna Judd. On his feet were sparkling navy stilettos. He was holding a plastic Captain America shield. I didn't even ask why.

"How do I look?" he asked.

"You look gorgeous," I said smiling. He really did.

"Thanks," he grinned.

He looked at the gray running shirt and black spandex that I had thrown on and asked, "Is that what you're wearing?"

We were headed to a local PrideFest event, and I was going to be running the Big Gay 5K (Yay!) for the first time. I hadn't made time that week to find something fun to wear, so I did rather blandly look like generic runner #71.

I stated the obvious: "No one will be looking at me."

He smiled a proud smile about that, clutched his shield, told me to "hurry up," and headed back to his bathroom to primp one more time.

I admit it, when Bo kept insisting that he and I had differences, he wasn't exactly exaggerating. Like I said before, he came from a very traditional, religious background ... and not only had I become a non-traditional, non-religious LGBTQ ally over the past few years, I also, technically, had a transgender son who likes drag.

Now, we don't care much for using labels around my house because souls are what matter these days, but for the purpose of explaining things here, I'll use just a few. Alex had come out as transgender the year before we moved to the sticks. Though born with female anatomy, he had *always* gender-identified as a male on the inside. "Coming out" was just his announcing and expressing that truth.

So ignore the body; it's just a meat suit for the soul.

He's a dude. He always was.

He's also a creative dude who likes art, music, and knitting (knitting needles are his "weapon of choice for the apocalypse" he likes to say) ... and he enjoys drag.

It was a gradual process to accept my son's coming out,

mostly because it was extremely confusing, as a parent, to know what to do with his old identity. It felt like I had gained a new, happier child in my life, but it also felt like I had lost the old one, whom I loved dearly … except that there was no goodbye, or death, to connect that loss to. That old identity just disappeared in a day.

It was a very difficult and strange process to go through. I had to create my own closure, which took time. When I did finally accept letting go of his old identity, I was able to embrace him as he is now, with my whole heart.

More important to Alex, though, I began binge watching drag queen reality shows, in display of my support.

He had introduced me to the concept one evening and I was hooked. After a couple of episodes, and a few glasses of wine, I was critiquing their fashion like I was a douchy guest judge— holding my wine glass in one hand, pointing at some queen's handmade gown with the other, and sneering, *"Oh for Chrissake, just surrender the glue gun already, bitch."*

There's lots of fun banter and hissing in drag, but there's also sweetness in the guys' personal stories. Many of them endured rejection or abuse growing up because they were feminine, yet here they were entertaining, being creative, and making a living doing what they love. Drag is not an easy or conventional profession to choose, so ironically enough, it takes serious balls to be a drag queen. They had my respect and I got emotionally attached to those bitches.

I supported Alex's interest in drag because, really, why not? It's just a fun form of entertainment in this world, that's all. It's not sexual deviance nor is it a representation of one's gender identity. It's just performance art and comedy. I enjoy it, too. Plus, we aren't much for the status quo around here.

Now, I was there when Alex was born, and I know that on paper he's a teenager, but behind that lanky frame, tousled multi-colored hair, and biker boots he's an old soul. In a past life he must have been the wise, pipe-smoking, smart-ass elder of a tribe somewhere. Like a tribal George Carlin. I'm sure his I.Q. is higher than mine, and he has a quirky, razor-sharp wit to match.

He's also a nice kid. He volunteers at the Humane Society, where he likes to take pictures of dogs that look like celebrities. He also likes to bake, and since it's just the two of us and we don't eat much, he makes cupcakes and takes them to the home-less shelter.

His usual attire is black jeans and a band t-shirt. My usual attire is cowboy boots, skinny jeans, and a perky, colorful shirt. We are the poster children for *Awkward Family Photos*. He keeps insisting he wants a gray, old-timey, striped swimsuit to wear this summer when he's with me—in my multi-colored bikini—just so we can get a photo looking like Carrie Underwood and Gomez Addams together at the beach.

He is an annoying teenager who smells bad at times and likes to make a loud, exaggerated Chewbacca-like groan when asked to empty the dishwasher. I embarrass him by doing dumb mom things like asking the person behind the counter at Panda Express, "Is the panda fresh today?"

We have a good thing together.

I don't think much about gender when I look at him any-more. He's just Alex. He's also the most intelligent, unique, funny person I will ever meet in my life, and I wouldn't change a thing about him. It's his soul that I love not his body, so I don't waste energy asking "why?" or wishing anything was different. It's not about me; it's about him. The most important thing is that he feels good about himself.

When I worked at Home Depot (before Alex came out), I remember a transgender woman who would come in to shop about once a month. She dressed in women's clothing and had a feminine hairstyle. She was also tall and had an Adam's apple. Though I was comfortable with the subject of homosexuality then, I still knew little about transgender and was completely ignorant as to why she went out dressed like she did. I am embarrassed that my initial, smug, shitty thought when I first saw her was, *"You know, you're not fooling anyone."*

I realize now that she wasn't *trying* to fool anyone, you dick.

She was just dressing to match how she felt on the inside, like a woman, in the same way I would. Here she was, being brave as hell to be herself like that out in public, and my first reaction was to mock her? What was wrong with me? I considered myself an open-minded, loving person, yet that reaction was just awful. Why did I react like that?

Because of Helen.

Ok, my ego. Which somewhere along the way I started to call Helen.

I have a large canvas painting of a cow in my bedroom. It's a modern-art-style cow with lots of bold colors. It's a closeup of her face only, leaning to one side, with one big eye looking down over my bed. One morning for some unknown reason, I woke up and said, "Good morning, Helen," and she has been Helen ever since. I started calling my ego Helen along the way, too. I suppose because it made it friendlier.

As I had been consistently practicing separating my ego from my soul, I had come to realize that my ego wasn't my enemy, it was just a naive, well-intentioned source of annoyance … kind of like a big-eyed cow named Helen staring at me while I sleep.

I suppose I wanted to put the woman in Home Depot down because it's a coping mechanism for feeling out of control. Feeling out of control triggers fear.

Fear triggers Helen to get defensive and to blame.

We are always labeling people at first glance, though we don't realize it. It's so natural … except when we see someone we can't instantly label. When we see someone who looks like a cross of both genders, it short-circuits the mind and fear kicks in. Our little brain label-maker, who works 99% of the time with no trouble on the subject, doesn't know what to do.

So, Helen kicks out blame and defensiveness because she is angry at the upset to her label-making control. That's what I was doing to that lovely woman.

I'm not going to fault anyone for having an awkward first reaction to seeing someone who can't be easily gendered. It's an old habit. It was mine, too.

Maybe I couldn't choose my first trigger reaction, but I certainly could choose my second. I began to run this process through my mind when I saw the woman the next time:

"Ok, eeeasy Helen, you can't easily gender this person, so I see you're getting upset.

No, Helen, it's not their fault.

Do they deserve my respect, not my criticism? Hells yes.
Is this internal nonsense my fault, not theirs? Hells yes.
Go back to the barn, Helen. Off you go."

The more I continued to recognize that my ego was the true source of my fear and defensiveness, the easier accepting others who are different than me became. Again, most of the unfair judgments I had made toward others in the past, like homosexuals, non-Christians, and now transgender people, were just my own ego-based fear reactions. The people I judged weren't a danger to me, they were just different.

Geez, Helen is paranoid.

That beautiful woman in Home Depot was certainly no threat to me. In fact, she is the braver soul.

Alex once described being out as transgender as "walking around with a tattoo on your forehead that says, *I'm different.*" By far, the most annoying thing is being misgendered by waitstaff and salespeople in stores. I know they mean no harm, but it drives us both crazy. When not 100% positive of someone's gender, it would be much better if people would just say "Hello" or a neutral "Hi, folks."

Enough with the "Hello, ladies." That one drives us both crazy—because he's not a girl, and I am no lady.

It's been one of my life's unexpected blessings to be the parent of a "different" kid. Alex has been my greatest teacher, reminding me that differences are a good and necessary thing. They're what keep life interesting and our world evolving. How painfully boring it would be if we were all exactly the same.

Winnie the Pooh says, "The things that make me different are the things that make *me.*"

Which is a simple bear's reminder that sometimes being different just means proudly being *yourself.*

## chapter eight

# of soulmates and psychics

My good friend Tracy prides herself on being the least athletic person in the history of competition. She made her grandfatherly high school swim teacher so uncomfortable with daily details of her menstrual cycle that he never made her get in the pool the entire semester, and she still got an A in the class.

She's in her forties now, but looks ten years younger than that. She has blonde hair, blue eyes, and a perfect smile. She is a pretty woman who turns heads, but her real beauty is that she is an un-athletic, happy realist.

She also steals condiments like I steal napkins.

I saw her recently and she told me that her husband, against all better judgment, had signed them up to play on an adult kickball league (has he met her?). She explained how she consistently gives her finest, last-place effort, sauntering to first base with careful timing to ensure she'll be thrown out and can go back to the dugout.

I mentioned karmic and soulmate relationships earlier; I think Tracy and I are two soulmates that met on the same vibe. When we met, the love was already there and we gelled instantly.

The more I accepted the idea of soulmates as real, the more it became clear to me who else in my life had been a soulmate. Tracy was the first that really stood out. A few others were old friends, a couple were new friends, and one was a family member, my Aunt Nancy.

My Aunt Nancy was the coolest person I ever knew. When I was a kid, she and her family would come visit us a few times a year. We'd wait all day for them to turn into our gravel driveway in their big-ass '70s station wagon—cousins, comic books, pop cans, and playing cards falling out of every window.

When Aunt Nancy's family was at our house, even for just a few days, it honestly felt like a happy place. I remember those summer evenings with such pleasure. The pack of us cousins, high on RC Cola and Pop Rocks, running through the sprinklers, while the adults sat at a wooden picnic table, talking and laughing. It was one of the few times I remember my parents laughing together.

She was a big woman, whose favorite outfit was red polyester pants (again, it was the '70s), comfortable sandals, and a red "I'm a Pepper" Dr Pepper t-shirt. She always colored her short hair a very unnatural tomato soup color, and to this day I still don't know what her natural hair color was.

Aunt Nancy had a great sense of humor and her kids, my cousins, were funny, too. They still tell stories of how she would cook with Spam when they were young. She would mold the Spam into the shape of chicken drumsticks for dinner, and her kids would harass her about it by yelling, *"She's playing God again! She's turning pig into chicken!"*

On a similar note, sometimes on the rare occasion that I cook, I'll make pasta and let Alex have a glass of watered-down wine with dinner. He loves it because it's his opportunity to yell at me, *"You're the Anti-Christ! You're turning wine into water!"*

Aunt Nancy would get a big laugh out of that.

Around the picnic table on those summer evenings, she would pull me up onto her lap, hug me, and say something sweet like, "Well hello, honey."

Then, as the adults talked, I'd lean back on her and she'd stroke my messy hair with her soft hands. It made me purr like a full-bellied kitten. Throughout my whole life she was the loving, supportive adult that I trusted the most. She is gone now, but I know she was a soulmate.

Another of my most precious soulmates is Alan, my seventh-grade crush.

We reconnected after my divorce and during his. We dated for a little while long-distance. We both knew it didn't have long-term potential, but there was something so healing about it that we didn't care. Alan was the first man in my life who showed real vulnerability. He raised the bar for me on how honest and open a man can be. Eventually our romance morphed back into friends, best friends. There will always be a platonic, soulmate love between Alan and me that is divine.

One karmic relationship worth mentioning came to me as a business partner. While other girls were reading *Little House on the Prairie* in grade school, I was reading *Mad* magazine. As a young orange, the toilet humor spoke to me. I liked sharp, slightly naughty cartoons.

I had first discovered this in my grandparents' basement in Cheyenne.

Whenever we came for visits, the adults shuffled all us kids into the basement so they could talk in peace. There were hardly any toys down there, which was fine with me, because all I ever wanted to do was read their collection of *The New Yorker* cartoon books on the bookshelves. They were compilation books of "The Best of 1956" or "The Best of 1960" cartoons from *The New Yorker* magazine.

The New Yorker cartoons are the crème de la crème of the cartoon world. They are known for their sophisticated humor and superior wit, and some had that slight naughtiness that I loved. They are where my comic snobbery, which I mentioned earlier, came from. I started with the best and worked my way down. By ten years old, I expected my cartoon punchlines to cut as smooth and sharp every time. That's why, when I said I thought Garfield was fucking stupid, I meant it.

He liked lasagna. Hilarious.

After my divorce, and after a few years of working at Home Depot, I went back into journalism. I was working at a suburban newspaper company as the marketing manager when they hired a well-known local cartoonist to do a weekly for them. He had drawn for a large Denver paper for almost thirty years. He was a Colorado icon and I was tasked with promoting that we now had him in our papers. He and I worked wonderfully together, and eventually he asked if I would run a company, creating and promoting products for him, which I did. We formed a partnership.

It was my dream job. The girl who grew up on *Mad* magazine and *The New Yorker* cartoons was now the president of a cartoonist's company!

His work was a fun and an easy sell. We worked with sports teams like the Broncos, the Rockies, and the University of Colorado. We did TV and radio promotions with the state's largest media outlets. The mental beast that I had become way back in my anxiety days came out as I made big decisions, took financial risks, and was not intimidated to chat with anyone we met.

The cartoonist and I had a lot of success working together. It was challenging and exciting, but it was also a lot of work. Eventually it felt like it was time for us both to move on, in different directions.

It was the job I left when I moved out of the city and to the sticks. I will always be grateful for him and that experience.

During my time running the cartoonist's company, I had my first experience with a psychic. An old friend from high school, named Renae, had come back into my life. We really hadn't communicated much in twenty years, but she called me out of the blue to see if she could come down from South Dakota and stay with me in Denver for a few days. Renae is cute and petite, with warm, chestnut brown hair and brown eyes. She has a wonderful laugh, and when she talks, she's got that Midwestern big "OOOHs" accent. She frequently starts her sentences with "Ya KnOOOW …" and it makes me grin every time. We picked up our friendship like no time had passed at all.

While she was visiting, we found that we had been on similar spiritual journeys. She had been studying Wayne Dyer, Deepak Chopra, and Eckhart Tolle at the same time I was. Our paths were very, very similar.

Renae told me that she had met a woman recently who was a psychic and asked if I'd be interested in going to a reading with her. I'd never been to a psychic (I wasn't even sure what they did) but I was curious, so I said why not. A few months later, we met again and went to a park, where we met a sweet, white-haired lady named Patsy.

We all sat at a picnic table ... which I thought was weird at first.

I guess I had assumed that she needed a special room to do a reading. It hadn't occurred to me that if someone has psychic abilities, it really doesn't matter where they are. She said she could have even met us at the mall, but that the park was quieter.

We took turns asking Patsy questions about our lives. "What do I need to know about my career path?" kind of stuff. She would close her eyes and just talk, answering what she could. Though I went into this voluntarily, my ego was telling me to be skeptical, so I put on my best poker face and was careful to say as little about myself as possible.

I wanted to stump the psychic, even if she did look adorably like Betty White.

She stumped me though.

I asked her to describe my kids' personalities, without knowing anything about them except their names. She described both, as they were at that time, to a tee. I was floored. If she was guessing at what she was saying, it was as big a miracle as her having psychic abilities. There's just no way she could have known the things she did.

My mind was absolutely racing afterwards as I asked Renae what the hell had just happened. Renae said that from what she understands, there are frequencies out there that psychics can tune in to (we can all do it, psychics have just mastered it), to communicate with the non-physical world.

It's as if Patsy tunes her mind's radio dial to the frequency that our souls are on (W.G.U.S—God/the Universe/Steve Radio), picks up what they're broadcasting, and then transmits it back out to us.

Though I had always believed that my personality would somehow melt into my soul and go on to some afterlife when I die, I had never really considered my soul overly relevant to *this* life.

And I'd *really* never considered that we can literally communicate with souls ... while we're still *alive*. But that's the only way I could explain what I had just witnessed.

Is there more going on in this world, on other frequencies, that we can't see?

An existential crisis is when an individual questions the very foundations of their existence. I spent the next three days having existential crisis #1.

One of the last things Patsy told us in our reading was that she had a strong vision of me getting a check in the mail. She said she could see me opening an envelope, and that in it, is a check of an amount much larger than what I am expecting.

Even though the whole experience had completely freaked me out and given me an existential crisis, I was glad to know I had this check thing going for me.

For a few weeks after our Patsy meeting, I ran to the mail every day looking for a certified letter from Publisher's Clearing House, but after a while I got distracted and forgot about the big check vision.

Things had gotten busy with the cartoonist's company. I had negotiated a contract with the state's largest grocery store chain to carry his calendar in 150 stores, and I was buried in logistics for months on how to make that happen. I was practically donating plasma to pay for things, and I never once felt confident that I knew what I was doing. I had to work through their giant parent company's system, just to get our one little product in Colorado stores, and it was a huge, confusing shit show on my end.

The whole time, I was under the impression that they were going to be paying us for what sold in stores, not for what they ordered. Watching the sales, I expected us to make about $65,000 from the deal, which would be paid at the end of the year.

When that time came, I kept checking our bank account for an electronic deposit from them, as everything we had done with them was electronic. I was starting to get nervous when it wasn't showing up as I expected. I had vendors to pay, and I was over my plasma donation limit for the month. We had a post office box that got used irregularly, so I decided to check there to see if maybe there was some correspondence from them on what was happening.

As I sorted through a pile of mostly crap, I saw an envelope from the parent company. Standing there in the post office, I ripped it open.

In it was a check.

It wasn't a check for $65,000. It was a check for $117,000.

They had paid us for the whole order, not just what had sold. It wasn't a mistake. I had misunderstood the agreement all along.

I shit myself. I sent Renae a picture of the check and she shit herself.

It was hard to reconcile that as coincidence for me. How she did it I don't know, but I now believed that Patsy was legit.

Months later the psychic/check experience was still sinking in. I was starting to accept the reality of these unseen, vibrational frequencies at work. Helen was going berserk over it, clinging to old beliefs and mooing relentlessly at me that it was all just coincidence and that any other possibility was me being nonsensical.

But really, isn't faith all about a higher power, souls, and believing in things we can't see? Doesn't the Bible say, "with God *all* things are possible"? Was there really anything about what the psychic did that conflicted with that?

Nah, I told Helen. Thanks for your concern, but I think it's fine. Shoo. Go have some hay.

## chapter nine

enter the warrior

The days were getting shorter and the nights cooler. It was now early fall, six months after Bo and I had first met, had our Florida trip, and broken up. I had gone back to online dating and had met a guy who I thought was finally a game changer. He was bright and funny, and we had a lot in common. We both liked jazz, sushi, mid-century modern, and Converse All Stars. We also totally agreed on social issues and spirituality. I was happy to be with someone who understood me so well.

"I think the fundamental core of every religion is don't be a dick," he said once.

Scholars can spend years analyzing millions of words on religion, but I think it does boil down to four words: Don't be a dick. Don't be a dick to others. Don't be a dick to yourself. It's not rocket science. Just play nice. My new guy and I agreed on that.

I met Bo for a "let's be friends" afternoon beer once while I was seeing my new fella. I told him I was excited about how much this new guy and I had in common. He told me that he was dating a nice woman from his church and that she, too, was everything he thought he was looking for.

We both agreed that we appreciated these people, and that they made sense for each of us, much more than the two of us ever would.

Yup.

Maybe it was true, but the more we talked, we both admitted the truth. These were great people, we could even say we *had* love for them, but we weren't *in* love with them, nor were we ever going to be.

It was a great lesson that we got at the same time: what's right on paper doesn't matter if it's not right for the soul. And maybe there's more to love than "having a lot in common."

We both ended those relationships a few weeks later.

I had an epiphany not long after that I needed to stop dating. I had done it enough. I was just chasing my tail.

I decided I needed to take some time to focus on myself and figure out if I was capable of a long-term relationship with anyone. *I was the common denominator* in my relationships, and maybe it was time to look closer at what I was contributing to them.

That evening I logged on to the dating site I had been using, to delete my profile. As my homepage came up, guess who popped up as a suggested "Top Prospect" for me? No shit, my favorite poop-talking, Harley-riding ginger. I shook my head and snorted in laughing disbelief,

"Are you shitting me, God/the Universe/Steve?"

I sent him a message about something in his profile. He messaged me back about mine, commenting, "You forgot to mention that you like long walks along the beach."

Then he called me and we talked for hours.

He told me again that he was sorry for the pain he had caused me while in his own pain and confusion.

I heard a deeper, different man that night.

We started to see each other again after that. We did a lot of simply hanging out and talking, especially on my patio on warm nights, while listening to music and looking out over the farm.

I told him more about me, my fears, and my strengths. He did the same, telling me more about his past, his passions, and his work as a firefighter.

Firefighters are unique people. It makes me sad that we (ok, I) treat them as sex objects, because they're so much more than that. They choose to run into situations that the rest of us flee from. They sign up to be there on humanity's worst days, and they see a lot of them. Bo has been there to cut down people who have hung themselves, he's watched an old man refuse to leave the side of his dead wife, and he's literally had to try and rescue people from burning vehicles—sometimes successfully, sometimes not. He'd experienced things up-close that I cringed to even hear about.

Thank a first responder. Hug them.

As he talked, I could tell there's a price that he's paid with his emotions for what he does. When you see that kind of trauma consistently, you have to compartmentalize your emotions or you can't keep doing it. I think all those years of compartmentalizing his emotions, out of necessity, affected his personal life, too. Emotions were hard for him. I noticed he'd either get quiet, or make a joke, when our conversations got too intimate.

I saw his feelings, though, in how he invited me to spend a day babysitting his two-year-old grandson with him, and in how he took me to the firehouse to meet his friends.

I could see it in the way we never lost eye contact when we talked for hours.

I also saw it in how he would gently kneel on the floor, facing me as I sat on the couch, and sweetly lay his head on my lap while we talked. We cared deeply about each other.

As the weeks went on, we would say goodnight for the evening and hug in precious silence for five or ten minutes. We just hugged—loving, warm hugs—hugs from the soul. It's hard to describe in words, but the best I can do is that it felt like "home."

He made comments during that time that some of the beliefs that he'd grown up with were "pretty antiquated." He also said he was starting to think God was more loving and less judgmental than he'd been taught growing up. He talked passionately about wanting to retire from firefighting, traveling, and living somewhere warm in the winter.

He also said to me, *"There is an underlying happiness when we are together."*

We talked over breakfast for hours some mornings about the difference between the ego and the soul. I tried to encourage him to consider that his insecurities are his ego, not who he really is.

In one of those conversations, he said the first thunderbolt thing that made me realize there was something different about our relationship.

He leaned in close to me, across the table, as he was talking about his desire to serve others. He looked me in the eyes, took my hands, and said, "I know this sounds weird, but I feel like I have the soul of a *warrior*."

As he said that, I instantly felt like something had *shocked my soul*.

A warrior.

Holy shit, I am brave. I am bold. I face things the m*%$er f&@#ing, s*#-of-a-b%#ch! hard way.

I am a warrior.

All that ego bullshit about our differences being "too much" could not defeat the fact that we each had the soul of a warrior.

He was being thoughtful at this time and I felt like being around him was bringing out the best in me. I felt light and inspired. It's when I started writing this book, still not knowing exactly what it was going to be about.

This was the time period when we were dating the second time, pretzel hugging, and talking about units and penetration that I mentioned at the beginning of the book.

And as I also mentioned back then ...

when he eventually left

for the second time.

As the weeks went on, I started to sense his fear again. I think our relationship was unexpectedly pulling out the best and worst of his emotions. I began hearing both love and doubts coming from him at the same time.

Things were good until he went to work for his 48-hour shifts. Then, during those hours apart, he'd start focusing on our differences again and talk himself into how this could never work. I began expecting a breakup conversation after every shift. For a couple of weeks, I talked him down from the ledge, but eventually he told me, with genuine sadness, that he just felt like he should go.

So, we broke up. *Again.* (This is when I kicked puppies and ate chips and dip in bed.)

After a few nights of nursing some heavy heartache, this time I found myself, surprisingly, not feeling so awful about it. Though it hurt to see him leave, if he had persistent doubts about us being happy together, there was really nothing more I could do about it.

So, I did something (shockingly mature) that I had never done before. I told the person I loved to go. I told him that I wanted him to walk into this relationship with peace, and that if he still had fears or uncertainty about it, then he should go, and that I understood.

My saying that was the second thunderbolt that told me this was no ordinary relationship … something huge had changed *in me.*

My ego had *exploded* the first time we broke up after our Florida trip. Remember the hinges falling off the door? At the time, I made sure it was only about me and my pain; it never even occurred to me that he had his own.

But as the year went on, that changed. Over our tailgate conversation and the "let's be friends" afternoon beers, I started to see him as a complex, conflicted soul.

The second time we dated, I realized there were no more deal breakers for me with him. I had grown to accept and care about him exactly as he was. I couldn't help him with what he needed, or it would have already happened. So, I told my fellow warrior to go and confidently told myself through some tears that hopefully we'd find each other again ... when the time was right.

It was mixed emotions like I'd never felt.

My ego hurt like hell, but my soul felt the most unexpected, unbelievable, serene, heavenly *peace* that I had ever experienced. I was reaching a depth of unconditional love that I didn't know existed. I would even dare to compare it to the same feeling that near-death experiences describe.

It felt like outer-body, crystal clear, pure, divine *bliss*.

A few weeks later that feeling had dissipated and I was having a heavy heart from just missing him, so I sighed and googled "Why men run."

Which is where I first found the phrase "twin flames."

## chapter ten

existential crisis #2

That night, God/the Universe/Steve decided it was time for me to understand what was really going on here. Spiritual people are firm believers that when something resonates with you, it's because you were supposed to be drawn to it. You're being called there.

As I skimmed the "Why men run" results, an article resonated with me. It was on a website talking about something called "twin flame" relationships and how there is a separation stage to those relationships. It described a series of stages that generally go from an initial meeting, to growing intensity, to hell in a handbasket, to separation (usually many times over), to eventual union again. As I read that article, I saw phrases like "magnet pull" and "feelings of home" appearing.

Then I found a YouTube channel on twin flames by a young Australian gal named Christabel Jessica. She was very articulate and intelligent, with no fruity stars and moon shit in her videos. She had pretty, long, blonde hair and looked like she could be a friendly bank teller during the day. In one of her videos, she described the same relationship stages that I had read about, and added that during the separation, it is typically the masculine energy that runs away. She described them as being overwhelmed by the depth of the emotions that meeting their soul counterpart triggers in them. She also said that as masculine energies, they have been taught by society to hold in their emotions.

"Emotions are frightening for these warriors," she added.

She actually used that word, *"warriors."*

Dayum.

She also described twin flame relationships as having a divine purpose or "mission." Ok, the word "mission" was fucking killing me because it sounded so painfully *Star Trek*, but I understood what she was saying. She and the other sites I found said that twin flames serve an important purpose—they are the catalysts for our awakening. They help us reconnect to our souls and unconditional love ... which helps with the (much needed) *mass* expansion of unconditional love is this world.

As much as it sounded a bit woo-hooey for even my spiritual palate, that was a *Star Trek* mission I could actually get behind. We could definitely use more unconditional love in this world.

As I watched more videos, I also heard it explained that twins are eternal soulmates that incarnate into human form for different life experiences. And Christabel added, that during past lives, they may have gained deep wounds that need to be healed before they can reconnect with their souls, and each other, in this lifetime.

"Wait, did she just say PAST LIVES?"

"MOO! MOO! MOOO! MOOOOO!" Helen began frantically prancing in circles.

Whoa. Past. Lives. Plural.

Wow. I hadn't expected that.

The Australian bank teller was suggesting that I have been reincarnating? I had never considered that.

I'd always believed that I was individually created at my conception.

I'd never considered that I had already been making the earth rounds for eternity.

Christ.

Make way for existential crisis #2.

Helen was now madly kicking up dirt and snorting at me that this was nonsense. She had me questioning if I was nuts, or just plain gullible, for even remotely contemplating that any of this could be real.

As I read other websites and found more videos, though, I found there are people all over the world describing this same twin flame relationship dynamic. Those sources said that twins can take the form of the opposite sex, the same sex, or even transgender. Bodies are irrelevant, because this is about souls and energies. And every source spoke about how these relationships are difficult ones.

This is because, while the souls may be recognizing and drawing each other close (hey, the soul knows what the soul knows), intellectually, emotionally, physically and spiritually twins may still be nowhere *near* the same vibe in life—and that contrast makes for a big, hot mess. Plus, once twins find each other, the connection shines a spotlight into the dark gap between their personality and their soul, which is painful and confusing ... especially if the gap is a big one.

The only relief, the only thing that will close that gap, the sources said, is to awaken and heal old wounds.

And if both can close their own gaps, they have the potential to become soulmates in harmony, rather than soulmates in chaos.

Going back to the ship analogy, think of it like a triangle: Bo and my's souls are bestie crewmates and on the same mothership, which is at the top of the triangle. Our smaller boat personalities are at the two, distant, opposite corners, out in choppy waters. The solution to solving our differences isn't to meet each other out in those choppy waters. It's to get closer to the soul mothership, where the water is always steady, and meet there.

As impossible as it sounded to Helen, part of me was starting to consider that this whole twin flame thing might have some truth to it. It all sounded too much like my and Bo's relationship for even my Spock logic to ignore.

Were we seriously soulmates *out of whack?*

Is THAT why this relationship felt so different?

Is THAT why I felt that shock to my soul?

And is THAT why I had experienced that surreal, unconditional love bliss ... even with him leaving?

Maybe twin flames *were* a real thing.

Ok then, so, for us to ever work, we each needed to get

into alignment with our own souls first and alignment with each other would follow. How hard could that be?

And what was this awakening and healing process that I kept hearing about?

What exactly did that mean?

This couldn't get any weirder, could it?

## chapter eleven

and then things got weirder

I sent Bo a link to one of the articles that I had found and a text that said, *"Holy shit! I think we're twin flames!"* I didn't expect a response from him because I knew it sounded absolutely nuts, but I sent it anyway.

I became such a whack job immediately after, that I'm glad he wasn't around.

My recognizing our soul connection must have triggered some cosmic force in the universe because this is the part where all kinds of unexplainable, weird-ass things started to happen.

The next day, as I was researching more, I found a woman in Denver who had written a book on her own twin flame experience. I wanted assurance that I wasn't imagining all of this, so I made an appointment to meet with her the next day. I also wanted to ask her more about what this healing process was that I kept reading about. A process that I noticed was frequently called doing "shadow work."

"The Shadow Aspect" is a phrase coined by the psychologist Carl Jung that refers to the unconscious aspect of the personality that we're not even aware of. Doing shadow work is pulling up deeply buried emotional garbage (that even we don't want to see) to heal and release. I was pretty sure there wasn't a *Healing Wounds from this Life and Past Lives for Dummies* book, so I wasn't sure how that was supposed to happen. Was it something I was supposed to initiate on my own? Was the universe going to send me a kit in a manila envelope in the mail? Before I even got to the appointment with the author to ask her that, I got my answer, and let me tell you, it had Helen going mad frickin' cow.

This is where I sound like I should be wearing aluminum foil on my head, but I'm just going to tell it like it happened.

That night as I was lying in bed, I had what could be described as a vision from a past life. It came to me as a clear memory, exactly like how I described the hypnotherapy experience of being in my mom's sewing room. It was like I was watching a movie. It felt very different from a dream. Dreams are usually some hodgepodge leftover of the day's events—people and places that are a distorted view of reality.

Dreams are more like seeing yourself at a wedding service, being conducted in a gas station, and in walks Bob Ross carrying your neighbor's cat. Dreams are weird. This was different. It was incredibly vivid and real, like recalling a memory, not a dream. I'd also say it wasn't like a dream because I don't think I have ever once dreamt of myself in another time period (have you?), and that's what this was.

Here's what I felt and saw in the vision …

It looked like ancient Rome or Greece, and it was inside a simple, primitive-looking dwelling. I saw a young couple, probably just teenagers, that I felt were Bo and me.

First, I saw us lying on a simple bed in a dark room with a small window above our heads. There was moonlight shining in the window. We were lying there in the quiet, embracing each other and softly crying. He had just told me that he would have to leave soon, that he was being called to go fight in some war. We accepted that he had to go, but the pain of him leaving was awful.

Next, I saw us in the same dwelling, but this time we were next to a table and it was daytime. He was sitting on a stool at the corner of the table, and I was standing in front of him, leaning forward and embracing his head in my arms, close to my chest. We were saying goodbye and not wanting to let go. I was crying hard. He had tears streaming down his face. On the floor watching us as we embraced was a toddler with blonde hair. He was our son.

The next thing I saw in the vision was Bo leaving, as I watched and sobbed from a doorway, holding our son on my hip. I watched the back of him as he walked down a path, away from the house, and into the sunlight.

I never saw him again. He never came back, and I never knew what happened to him.

I felt the moment like it was happening, and just as it became too painful, I snapped out of it. When I woke up, I had the feeling of a panic attack for a few moments. Then, as I lay there in complete confusion over what the hell had just happened, I began to feel physical sensations of what, I later read, other people describe as symptoms of awakening. I felt a pleasant tingling sensation around the left side of my chest that felt internal. To be honest, the best way to describe it is that it felt like ... well ... an orgasm of the soul. It did. It felt like a tingling followed by a huge, radiating release.

Eventually I fell asleep.

I now understood how this healing process was going to work. It wasn't a workbook and six-week CD course; it was just going to happen.

Existential crisis #1 was when I witnessed the Betty White psychic connect to that other frequency.

Existential crisis #2 came when I considered that I am reincarnating.

And now I had just experienced for myself something far beyond the scope of the only reality I had ever known.

Hello existential crisis #3.

I went to Denver and met the twin flame author that afternoon. She was a pretty lady, probably in her late fifties, with shoulder-length, dark brown hair. She met me at the door of her condo wearing maroon stretch pants and a long, cozy sweater. She was very friendly and invited me in to sit on her couch and talk. I hadn't slept much and was still in the depths of existential crisis, so I must have looked like Beetlejuice, but she didn't seem to notice. She had a calm demeanor that I was appreciating so much. I was so grateful to be sitting down with someone who could possibly explain to me that what I was experiencing was real and reassure me that I wasn't losing my mind.

We chatted for a bit and I told her about the vision that I had had the night before. She assured me that what I had experienced is normal during spiritual awakening. She said memories from past lives can surface in visions, exactly like I had experienced. She also validated the physical symptoms that I described.

"All normal. It's your chakra opening," she said. That was good to hear … though I had absolutely no idea what she was talking about.

I started to describe to her the details of the vision I had seen of us saying goodbye. She listened intently and stared at the ground as I talked. I told her how in the vision, I never knew what happened to him.

She interrupted me, looked up, and said, "He died. He died fighting."

I stopped for a minute and took in what she said. He had died.

We talked some more about past lives in general. She confidently assured me, like it was no big deal, that reincarnation is very real. She said that when we are drawn to certain places, cultures, or history in this life, it's often because we have had a past life experience there.

As she got up to get some water, I thought to myself for a minute of other things in my life that may have resonated with me because of this possible past life. The primitive dwelling in my vision honestly reminded me of *The Flintstones*, my very favorite cartoon, and I've always joked that Barney Rubble was my perfect man. Bo definitely had a Barney Rubble quality to him—stocky, full head of hair, compassionate, and funny. Me, the queen of logic, was sitting there, rationalizing that I had always loved *Barney Rubble* because he reminded me of my soulmate twin flame.

The existential crisis paused for a minute and I laughed.

This was nuts. Absolutely nuts.

As we wrapped up our session, she gave me her card and showed me to the door. I gave her an appreciative hug and got in my car to drive back to the sticks. As I drove out of the city, I tried to process what we had discussed. Was the vision a real memory from a past life? Is that possible? Or was it just an incredibly detailed dream that I created? And if so, why did it feel so different than a regular dream? And what the hell is a chakra?

My mind was racing and I really wanted to cry, but I had to go to my son's parent-teacher conferences immediately after I got back.

It seemed a bit surreal to have to sit with a science teacher and talk about missing assignments when what I really wanted to say was, *"Excuse me, can we please do this another time? I really need to go mourn the death of my teenage warrior lover, who died a few thousand years ago … and I just found out today."*

I made it through the conferences then drove around the countryside bawling over how crazy I was feeling. That night I had the orgasm of the soul happen again.

The next day, I was still in an existential crisis fog, but I could function. I felt like I wanted to tell Bo about the past life vision I had. We hadn't talked for a few weeks. It was a Saturday afternoon. I sent him a text casually saying ...

"Hey, I had a weird past life vision about us yesterday that I'd like to share with you. Let me know if you want to hear about it." (smiley face emoji)

He messaged me back. He said he had met a friend earlier

and that he was just hanging out, having a beer, and eating something downtown.

He must have been a little drunk, because he actually said "Ok" to that bizarre text.

And now that I was experiencing new realities, I was also firmly believing that nothing "just happens" and that it was part of a divine plan that he was a bit tipsy that afternoon. I think what I was going to tell him was best received with a somewhat "lowered resistance."

I picked him up and we headed to a park, where we sat together on the same side of a picnic table by some pine trees. It was late fall, but it was 80 degrees, sunny, and beautiful outside.

I asked him if it was fine if we talked about spiritual stuff.

His lowered resistance said, "Ok."

I explained twin flames and soulmates to him. When I was done with that part, I told him about my dream of seeing us as a young couple and his leaving. He concentrated on my words and stared at the table as I talked.

When I was finished, he didn't have a passionate break-through saying, "Yes, I see it too!" but nor did he say, "That is batshit crazy, you horrible devil woman!"

He just looked up, speechless and confused, stared into my eyes for a long minute, and then lovingly hugged me tight. It might very well have been an "I'm really going to miss you in the mental institution" hug, but I didn't care.

We sat hugging at the picnic table in silence for quite a while. When we finally pulled back, he gently brushed my bangs to one side and said, "Let's go get a beer."

"God yes, please," I replied.

I drove us to a local craft brewery. He had forgotten his wallet so I said, "Don't worry about it," and reached into mine to pay. Which sent him mini apeshit. He likes to pay. It's just a Southern thing that he does and I appreciate it, but I insisted that he let me get a couple of $5 beers this once. He relented. Standing together, I smiled and said to the bartender, "I'll have a Nitro and please get my lady friend here whatever he would like."

He laughed and told me I was a "ha ha funny girl" as we took our beers out to an empty patio. We relaxed out there by ourselves, taking turns picking out favorite songs on our phones. We both put our feet up, and just enjoyed the weather and being in each other's presence.

Later as I pulled up his street to drop him off, before he said anything, I offered, "This was beautiful, thank you. Go do what you need to do. Hopefully, I'll see you again soon."

He looked sweetly at me with appreciation, exhaled, and said, "Thank you. Thank you for understanding that." Then we hugged tightly and said goodbye, like we didn't know if we'd ever see each other again ... for the tenth time.

I knew this was still *way* too much for Barney Rubble to process.

This was a million spiritual miles away from anything he'd ever heard. It had left him speechless.

I had been slowly spiritually awakening for a few years, and *I* was an emotionally chaotic, flaming mess over this soulmate reality and the unexplainable experiences that were coming with it.

He was definitely not ready for any of this.

As with all twin flame relationships, they are the catalyst for our awakening.

Apparently, I was going first.

He was really going to owe me for that $5 beer.

there isn't enough money or beer in the world ...

Meeting your twin flame soulmate, by divine design, accelerates one's spiritual awakening, though there really is no concrete definition of what spiritual awakening is.

Based on what I experienced next, the worldly description would be that I went through a psychotic episode or a mental breakdown, but I'm sticking with spiritual awakening.

I was now having frequent orgasms of the soul, shadow wounds surfacing daily, and was feeling brutally lost as to who I was and the entire structure of the universe.

I assumed that meant the awakening process was in full swing.

It came on fast and, truthfully, it felt like complete and utter hell.

Starting from the time I went to see the author, for about a month, I felt like I was in an existential fog and was having the shadow work healing come in weird cycles every day.

At least once a day I would start feeling down about something and want to cry. Eventually, a thought would trigger in my mind of what was making me feel so awful. It was always some painful memory from the past.

Once I connected the feeling to that past memory, I would then really feel the emotion, *cry a shitload,* and then feel an intense release of that negative energy. The releasing felt good when it happened. A nice relief would come over me for a few hours or until the next day, when it would happen again. I was not a pretty picture while all of this was happening, but it felt like every day was slowly moving me upward, in an even bigger spiral, toward my overall healing.

The wounds that surfaced varied. Some were family memories. Others were about friendships. One about a horrible boss came up. There were ample wounds from my romantic relationships, as well. It ran the gamut of things. Ultimately, I began to see that the common thread every time was that unworthiness and shame that I took on when I was young. It was the same shame that I had addressed during my June Fucking Cleaver anxiety days, but it now was coming up from even deeper depths, not to be examined just intellectually ... but to be emotionally *felt* and *released*.

Though the healing cycles were not as bad once I began to know what to expect (and that they would eventually pass), there was a miserable side effect happening. I felt like I was having a total identity crisis. As I was separating from lifelong wounds that I'd always identified with, I felt like I didn't know who I *was*. If I wasn't all those old stories anymore, than who was I? I was in identity limbo and it was horribly uncomfortable.

In addition, as I was now experiencing mental and physical things that I couldn't explain, I began to feel very isolated, like none of my friends or family would ever believe or understand what I was going through.

I felt like Harry Potter. A wizard in a world of Muggles. Destined to live under the stairs.

Plus! On top of the identity crisis and unexplainable experiences, I was also processing a complete paradigm shift that God/the Universe/Steve is much more infinite in intelligence and interactive with us than I ever imagined!

It was a lot for my well-intentioned, protective cow to process and she let me know it. It felt like a cage match between my ego and my soul. It was just plain mentally and emotionally painful.

So no, my spiritual awakening/psychotic episode was no picnic in the park. I've heard other people call the experience "The Dark Night of the Soul."

Yeah, it was as fun as that sounds.

But it did progress.

And I found things that helped.

The best advice I found was to surrender to it. That didn't mean give up, it meant lean into the discomfort and stop fighting it. My mind was evolving to a higher level of conscious understanding of my soul and the universe, and the mental pain was coming from my ego *resisting* that evolution of thought (it should really be called "The Dark Night of the Ego").

The sooner I started saying, *"Ok. God knows this is something that I can't explain, but I'm just going to let it happen,"* the more peace I felt.

I also made a point to practice self-care and self-love. Despite how awful I felt, I gave myself praise for how well I was doing. I bought myself flowers. I forced the cat to cuddle with me and I walked a lot. A lot. A lot. Just feeling my feet on dirt or grass helped so much.

I also put a bulletin board next to my bed and filled it with positive messages that would help me feel not so lost and alone. My favorite quote was from Eckhart Tolle, the teacher with whom I started this journey, from his book *A New Earth* ...

"Many people who are going through the early stages of the awakening process are no longer certain what their outer purpose is. What drives the world no longer drives them. Seeing the madness of our civilization so clearly, they feel somewhat alienated from the culture around them. Some feel that they inhabit a no-man's land between two worlds. They are no longer run by ego, yet the arising awareness has not yet become fully integrated into their lives. Inner and outer purpose have not merged."

That is exactly how it felt, like being in a hellish no-man's land. But as Winston Churchill once said, "If you're going through hell, keep going."

## chapter thirteen

helen, meet keith

About a month later, the healing cycles were mellowing. They were still happening and miserable, but the whole experience seemed to be slowing down. I found myself wanting to write down what I had just been through, for either your entertainment, or for my case file at the group home.

The past month had been painful and bizarre, and I was trying to get some perspective on what I had just been through. It felt like what needed to break in me … had broken. I had emotionally vomited up so many old wounds that I felt exhausted. I was still feeling the identity crisis, but I began feeling less lost and, thankfully, more like a blank slate.

Ok, so I was going through spiritual awakening. But what exactly was I "awakening" to?

For starters, I was now having complete clarity that we are not separate from God or each other. We are all human extensions of an infinite, intelligent energy source that is God/the Universe/Steve. What makes up you and me is what makes up God. It's all the same. *Everything* is divine.

I think this is what Jesus meant when he said, "the Kingdom of God is within you," and when the Apostle Paul asked, "Don't you realize that all of you together are the temple of God and the spirit of God lives in you?"

Secondly, I was awakening to the reality that I am literally an eternal being. I was not created at conception and dropped here for a one-time-only life experience, with eternity to start "later." I am continuously reincarnating, and evolving, with every life experience I have. This isn't my first rodeo. (I am going to go ahead and say it this time because there's a reasonable chance that I have been to a rodeo in a past life, and I've decided that counts.) When God said, "I knew you before I formed you in your mother's womb," he meant it. I existed *before* my conception.

Thirdly, I was remembering who I really am, which is simply unconditional love. I learned fear. I learned labels. I learned hate. Spiritual awakening is unlearning old beliefs and tipping the scale from living through the fear-based ego ... back to living as the soul. I was going home to who I really was.

These were the things I was now awakening to.

What had previously felt like theories in my mind were now realities, like oxygen and gravity. I now understood that I am not a human having a spiritual experience, but rather, I am a *spiritual* being having a human experience.

I'll admit, I was pissed at the universe for how painful the past month had been. The Dark Night of the Ego will make anyone grumpy. But I was starting to get a glimpse of the good that was coming from all of this. There was a sense of freedom emerging from it.

I reached out to Bo and asked him if I could read him the beginning of this book. It had been a few months since our afternoon in the park, when I had told him about the past life vision. He knew I was writing a book, but he didn't know that it was about this twin flame/awakening experience.

Hell, neither did I, until it kept progressing.

Right before I reached out to him, I had a memory come to me of a comment that he had made during our last month of dating. We were standing in his bedroom, sorting through some paperwork, when he said to me that his favorite number was 33 … which is also mine.

That was strange, we said at the time and then let it go.

After that memory came up, I googled numerology to see if there was a spiritual meaning behind the number 33. Numerology is the belief that numbers are signs used by the universe/spirit world to communicate with us. It's been used for centuries all over the world by different cultures and spiritualities. I found 33 to usually mean "master teacher" and/or "Jesus," because Jesus was a master teacher. The Bible says Jesus was 33 when he died, that he's part of the three-part trinity, and that he rose on the 3rd day. Jesus is all about 3s.

Given all the other strange things that had happened since we had met, I now couldn't accept that it was just coincidence that both our favorite number was 33. There's just no way.

He agreed to meet, run some errands, and find a place where I could read to him. We had a nice time catching up as we drove around town. Keith was with us. Keith is what Bo annually names his No-Shave-November moustache. Keith is a very machismo ginger moustache. Bo grows Keith long, down to his chin, so for the month he looks like a '70s truck driver/porn star.

As I sat in the passenger seat of his truck, I told him that some *seriously* weird things had started happening to me since we met—things that were hard to explain as anything but spiritual.

I said to him, "*Look, I'm fully aware that I sound like a lunatic for what I'm saying*, but I want to talk more about this twin flame thing. It's just not going away."

He said, "All right."

I told him that I was really starting to believe that we are soulmates, which means we have known each other in many lifetimes and that we have a purpose, a *Star Trek* love mission if you will, to awaken and spend the rest of our lives teaching about spirituality and unconditional love.

... "and all of this was confirmed by an Australian bank teller on YouTube."

"What's so hard to believe about that?" I laughed.

He looked at me and laughed aloud but had no words to respond. I brought up 33 being both our favorite number and asked him what he thought about that. He said he didn't know what to make of it. We stopped at a hardware store, and as we walked through the aisles, I told him that 33 had been my favorite number since childhood. He said the same.

We paused for a second, as he asked a young sales clerk what aisle the carabiners were in.

"Aisle 3," the fella responded. Of course.

We made another stop nearby at one of those dollar-for-everything-one-buck-mart stores, for me to pee and for him to find something to snack on. I met him in line, where he had a can of chips in his hand and was getting ready to pay.

I looked at the can. It had a Christmas motif on it. Considering where we were, I assumed it was from the previous Christmas, almost a year ago.

"Those are probably from last Christmas," I whispered.

He smiled at the cashier as he lay them on the conveyor belt, and out of the side of his mouth whispered back, "Only if we're lucky."

As we drove around munching on stale chips, he commented that he had changed over the year, as well, and admitted that it had started when I came into his life, too. He said he was still going to his same church, but that the judgmental, white-haired Gandalf God wasn't exactly how he saw God anymore.

We found a brewery so we could have a pint and I could read him the beginning of this book. Yes, breweries are a constant theme here. Colorado is the Napa of beer. We love exercise, dogs, the mountains, tattoos, and craft beer. It's the way of our people.

We took a few beers and my laptop outside to a back-patio area, where I read him the first two chapters of this book. It was surreal and fun to be reading him the account of our first date. We were both laughing and enjoying it. When I was done, he smiled, said it was great, and gave me a big bear hug.

Later out in the parking lot, as we got ready to part, I suddenly derailed into a screeching, tipped-over, flame-bursting train wreck. I just snapped and started to cry, ranting resentment at him over how unfair it was that I had been enduring past life flashbacks, existential crises, and mental hell in this stupid joint venture of ours, while he was out pretty much living his normal life. I don't know what I wanted ... for him to feel worse or for him to make me feel better.

Confused and unsure of what to say, he rubbed my arms with sympathy and simply offered, "*I'm sorry. Oh Julie, I'm just not there yet.*"

I paused and sniffled.

Wait a minute ... did he just say *yet?*

Was there still a chance that he might awaken, too?

And how come when I read him what I wrote about us being twin flames, did he not voice any resistance to it?

Hmm. Could at least *some* part of him feel we were soul-mates, too?

We thanked each other for the day and parted ways, leaving it open as to when we'd talk again.

Later at home, I realized my emotional train derailment meant that I still had some more healing to do because I was letting my well-being be controlled by his behavior—behavior that was out of my control.

I was wanting him to hurry up and awaken so *I* would feel better, which was senseless on my part.

He just was where he was, and he was only responding from the level of conscious understanding that he was capable of. Whether he was going to have the same awakening experience wasn't up to me. That was going to be between him and him. I needed to start accepting that our experiences were different ...

and that he may or may not wake up, too.

And I had no doubt that insecure Keith was going to fight tooth and nail to hold Bo to his lifelong beliefs and fears.

Keith? Yes, I decided to name Bo's ego Keith. Helen, meet Keith. Keith, meet Helen.

Keith, to me, is sort of like Uncle Rico from the movie *Napoleon Dynamite*. He means well, but he's got an overinflated sense of confidence.

"How much you wanna make a bet I can throw a football over them mountains?" Uncle Rico likes to brag.

He's a grown man who lives in a van, with a bad bowl haircut and even worse moustache, who dresses like a little boy from the '60s. His proudest accomplishment was being the high school quarterback. You can't hate Rico, he's harmless. He's got your back. He's just annoying about it, like Helen.

So, this twosome just became a foursome: Julie, Bo, Helen, and Keith.

Bo's beliefs ran deep and he'd never even heard of his ego until he met me. For him to awaken out of Keith and close the gap with his soul would be like coming out of neck-high quicksand for him. I needed to stop relying on that to happen for me to ever feel normal again.

Geez, could I really do that? This relationship was a complete life-changer for me. My letting go of any expectations with this was going to be hard.

It was my quicksand.

***

## chapter fourteen

the breakup

One morning not long after that, I woke up and decided it was over. I couldn't take it anymore. All the unknowns were killing me. I was done.

I broke up with Taco Bell.

I did. I also broke up with every meat product in my house and every product that I assumed came inhumanely from animals, from nacho cheese to eyeliner. It all got dumped one morning in a revelation of disgust as the cats watched and cheered me on.

I had read other people say the same thing happened to them during awakening—they have a new awareness about how precious animals are, and that the idea of eating them or using products that are tested on them, suddenly becomes gag worthy. It was true. It hit me overnight.

In the past, I had turned a blind eye to where my meat came from or how my products were tested, usually in the name of cost and convenience. I was busy and I loathe (it's not a strong enough word) the grocery store, so grabbing something on the road had become common; plus, it was how I got all my napkins.

I had always had a nice separation in my mind between my burgers and an actual cow by using the word "beef" instead of saying "cow." But now, the thought that I was ordering a "cow quesadilla" had me completely green. I was looking at animals differently. That disconnect wasn't there anymore, and I felt like they had more value than I had ever given them credit for.

We had gotten Oliber the cat the day after we moved to the sticks. He's a ginger tabby and the most handsome feline you'll ever meet. He's a thoughtful bugger, too—he makes sure to provide me company every time I sit on the toilet, without fail. After a few months, we decided to get him a friend (and um, yes, I'll get around to telling the landlord). We found a tiny gray cat at the shelter that Alex named "Beans." Beans is full grown and a whopping four pounds. She's just a live cat toy for Oliber. She holds her own when they play though. After just a few months they started to snuggle together, and now they seem to be best friends. Awakening made me no longer want to eat anyone's best friend.

Similarly, I found myself feeling the same way about the planet and nature. I suddenly no longer wanted to take this beautiful blue ball for granted, so the great product dump also included meticulously emptying every container and properly sorting every single recyclable.

It was a busy morning.

Other strange things happened, too, as I continued to awaken. I was really getting called to notice "synchronicities." Synchronicities are those coincidences that aren't coincidences. Numbers, names, and similarities that show up and grab our attention.

Numbers, names, and similarities that I believe are affirmations from God/the Universe/Steve that they're there.

And yes, I know I sound like an aluminum foil-head for saying that, but I don't care. I'm going to wear my aluminum foil proudly. I may even shape it like a swan.

I suspect there will be three groups of you out there on this subject:

1. Those who believe these synchronicities mean absolutely nothing and are purely coincidence. If that's you, I'm really surprised that you're still reading this book.

2. Those who say maybe it's the universe, maybe it's coincidence, but I'll play along.

3. Those who are already wearing aluminum foil swans on their heads and can't wait to read more.

I wasn't deliberately looking for synchronicities, they just started to appear in my awareness as I was going through awakening.

The biggest one was that I began seeing certain numbers *everywhere*.

It started with 33s.

In stores, my total would be $33.33, I'd get 33 cents back, I'd end up in aisle 33, or my claim number would be 33. If I saw a jersey anywhere, it would always be the number 33.

Then 11:11s joined in.

Alex and I were at the grocery store one day and I (paying no attention) picked up a box of cookies called Pocky. When we got home later, I saw the box read, "National Pocky Day is 11-11!"

I also noticed the apartment number and building number that I lived in added up to 11/11. And at least once, if not twice a day, I would impulsively glance at my phone at 11:11.

Those are just a *few* examples of what I was seeing all day, every day. My eyes were being drawn to 33s and 11:11s on every damn clock, billboard, t-shirt, drive-thru, road sign, and license plate in Colorado. It was almost annoying. I tried seeing if I could pick another number and have it still happen. I tried to look for 18 for a few days.

It didn't work. I was still being drawn to 33s and 11:11s constantly.

And feel free to explain this.

As all of this was happening, I was drawn to look back at old texts between me and Bo. There was one from the fall, before either of us had even heard the phrase twin flames. We had been texting back and forth about movies and in one text he said to me,

"We're twins. But you're the hotter one. There's always a hotter one."

I thought at the time that he must have been quoting a movie or something, so I just replied "lol." When I saw it those months later, I sent it back to him and asked him why he said that. We had never once referred to ourselves as, or joked about us being, twins.

He replied, "I don't know, just being silly I guess."

He just randomly called us *hot twins* right before I discovered we are *twin flames*?

Again, there are no coincidences in my book and like I said, this is my book (the book that I was told in my mind to start writing a few weeks *before* I even knew I would be going through this experience).

But you get to decide for yourself.

Just make sure you recycle that aluminum foil.

## chapter fifteen

(penis rock is no coincidence either)

Helen, with best intentions, kept cautioning me that I shouldn't tell people that I was going through this spiritual awakening experience. I was wrestling with sounding like a complete weirdo or admitting to myself and others that I was now a total believer in what I once would have called, hippie dippy bullshit.

I was getting tired of feeling sheepish about it, so I finally decided I needed to just own it. It was time to come out of the closet about being a spiritualist, past lives and all. Harry Potter was lonely under the stairs and wanted to be out in the world again. So, I started looking for places where I could connect with other people with whom I could have conversation about what I now understood and had been experiencing.

My old friend Renae (the one who took me to the Betty White psychic) invited me to join her for a monthly meeting for spiritual people in South Dakota. So, I took a quick road trip north to check it out. The meeting was led by a friend of hers named Jason. Jason is a dark-haired, good-looking, thirty-year-old married dad. He works for a power company during the day. He swears a lot. I liked him right away.

We met at the clubhouse of a nice, new apartment complex in town. There were probably forty people at the meeting and not one of them looked airy-fairy or weird. They were friendly older people, middle-aged women, a few married couples, and college students. I sat between Renae and a tall, fresh-faced engineering student named Keegan. We chatted for a few, and he told me about his growing up in a tiny town in eastern South Dakota. Keegan was a cool kid. I was liking this already.

After everyone settled into chairs that were gathered in a big circle, Jason began the meeting. It was leading up to Christmas, and he wanted to talk about how to protect our inner energies during the craziness of the holidays. He had us close our eyes, and in a calm voice told us that we were going to create a protective layer around ourselves.

As we all took deep breaths together, he told us to slowly put an invisible layer of protection around our bodies, starting at our feet and working our way up. It could be anything—like a bubble or a coat of paint. Whatever we wanted, whatever color we wanted, he said.

As I sat there with my eyes closed, I took a few deep breaths. In my mind I saw myself slowly bending over my feet, and I saw yellow, a bright, sunshine yellow. I felt myself slowly pulling that yellow up both legs, over my waist, up my chest, and finally over the top of my head. I smiled and leaned back when I was done, feeling satisfied and safe in my big yellow suit.

Then my mind saw me from the outside, looking back at myself.

I was wearing a yellow Teletubby suit.

What the hell?

I opened one eye and looked around the room. Everyone else was sitting peacefully, smiling, and picturing their protection suits. I felt like I was actually in a Teletubby suit. I looked at Renae with my one open eye. She happened to look at me.

"What?" she whispered.

"I'll tell you later," I answered.

Jason finished the exercise. He told us to open our eyes and asked how it went for everyone. A few people described their suits. I confessed my vision.

"Well, Teletubbies are creepy as hell. They could repel anything," I told the group.

Though I wasn't feeling like such a lonely wizard after the group that night, Helen would still wander in circles around me, shaking her head and mooing at me that spirituality was weird. I recognized her doing it, so I kept looking for other ways to calm her concerns.

As I started my drive from South Dakota back to Colorado, I passed the Pine Ridge Indian Reservation. I respect the native people of South Dakota (and this whole country), and it saddens me that their culture, land, and rights have been shit on horribly in American history.

The Black Hills of South Dakota are sacred land to the

Lakota Sioux, and in 1868 the government signed The Sioux Treaty, guaranteeing the Lakota ownership of the Black Hills. A great gesture ... except that gold was later found in the hills, and the land was seized back by the government only nine years later, in 1877.

Not only were the Black Hills taken back from the Sioux, about sixty years later, white men decided to carve other white men in the rocks there, creating Mount Rushmore. Now, I don't dislike Mount Rushmore, because it really is a special thing. I've been there dozens of times.

I just don't love where it is.

I mean, we can't exactly *move* it, but in hindsight, wasn't it incredibly disrespectful to carve white leaders into their sacred land?

There's a road around the side of Mount Rushmore that takes you right under George Washington's nose. It's a real hit with the tourists. But I'll let you in on a secret ... if you go about a mile or two farther down that road, on your right, you'll also pass under what locals call "Penis Rock."

Penis Rock has got to be the most perfectly phallic natural rock formation in North America, maybe even the world. It looks like a smooth, wonderfully erect, circumcised penis, and it's literally around the corner from Mount Rushmore. You don't even have to be an orange to find it ridiculously splendid. I like to think it's the Native Americans well-played response to the white man taking back and carving up their sacred hills. Its location is no coincidence if you ask me.

Wow. Did I really just find a relevant way to work Penis Rock into this story? Do I smell a Pulitzer?

Anyway, my original point was that as I passed Pine Ridge, I thought about how many indigenous people, for centuries, have believed in reincarnation and a direct connection to an interacting spirit world. In my culture, it is generally considered weird to do so, but to billions of other people around the globe, it would be weird *not* to. So why had it been such a struggle for me to admit out loud that I now believed it as the truth?

It's unfortunate that our current ego-dominated culture is so skeptical of spirituality outside of religion because I was now experiencing unconditional love beyond what I ever imagined, and I wished masses of others could feel it, as well.

It's too bad I let Helen waste my time thinking it was hippie dippy bullshit all those years.

Oh well, what really mattered was that I was awakened now.

I got a little tattoo during all of this that simply says in typewriter font, "yet."

I look at it and think, maybe I haven't seen and done everything I'd like to do, and maybe this world isn't the more peaceful place that it could be. But I believe that it can happen.

It just hasn't happened, yet.

And maybe someday more people will recognize their egos at work and open their minds to spirituality like Renae, her friend Jason, fresh-faced Keegan, and I had.

And maybe someday in our culture, believing in an interacting spirit world, reincarnation, and our oneness with God/ the Universe/Steve will be less of a social oddity and more of a social norm.

Maybe someday.

It just hasn't happened … "yet."

## chapter sixteen

is this the real life or is this just fantasy?

As I got comfortable in the tan leather office chair across from him, I asked my therapist, Wes, "Is there any possible psychological explanation for this deep connection to Bo?"

I had been to Wes in the past and had called him again to get some help with my shadow work. He's about forty, wears hipster glasses, and usually meets with me in khakis, a colorful button-up shirt, and leather loafers. I like Wes. I value his help and insight. He's extremely intelligent and is open to the idea that psychology overlaps with spirituality.

He's also a snappy dresser.

At times, I was honestly still questioning if this was all just a bizarre delusion made up by some dysfunctional part of my mind.

"Well, the fact that you're even asking me tells me you're self-aware and not hallucinating," he replied.

Good point. I told you I like Wes.

Leaning forward in my chair, I cupped my hands and asked, "Is it possible that a perfect storm of two dysfunctional people could create a catalyst for all of this sudden shadow work healing that I'm going through?"

Twitching his pen in one hand, he answered, "Well, it's normal for a person to have an attraction and connection to another that mirrors their own insecurities and wounds so closely."

I could understand what he was saying. I could accept that finding our emotional mirror in this life could be the catalyst for childhood wounds to come up, which could, yes, land one in the therapist's office wanting to make some changes

But textbook psychology still couldn't explain the orgasms of the soul, the spiritual awakening symptoms, and the synchronicities that I was seeing everywhere. That's where this crossed out of pure psychology into something else—something beyond conventional understanding.

Wes acknowledged those points as well.

After some good discussion, I told Wes, "Ultimately, I guess the perfect label or definition really doesn't matter. Whatever it is, it's just there. I feel it. Call it twin flames, call it the perfect storm of dysfunction with a twist. All I know is, I've experienced all these changes because of some connection between him and me. And as much as it's been total hell at times, I have to admit,

I'm grateful."

I hadn't seen Bo and Keith since the day I read them the book and had the train wreck in the parking lot months earlier. He had recently started dating someone new, yet we still kept in irregular communication with each other at times. I suppose I kept the communication open, even with him dating, because I was, admittedly, still very curious to see if he was showing any signs of awakening. Under normal relationship circumstances— i.e., ones that don't come with multiple existential crises and a complete paradigm shift of the universe—I would have stopped talking and moved on by this point.

One day I said to him, "Look, I know it still sounds beyond belief to you that we could have a *literal* soul connection. I understand, The idea of us being twin flames still seems implausible to me some days, too. But looking at the changes we've both experienced since we've met, and all the synchronicities, it's starting to seem impossible to me *that we're not."*

His response was a confused, "My mind can process only so much at a time."

Again, no "yay," yet no "nay" from him on the subject.

Another time, he brought up a remark that I had made on the hinges-off-the-door breakup night. I had apologized for my behavior that night month ago.

"We hurt each other that night. Was my behavior really unforgivable?" I asked him.

"No," he admitted, sounding frustrated with himself.

Then I asked him something that opened the floodgates and washed Keith downstream.

"Then what, exactly, is the block that keeps you from

forgiving and letting it go?"

Woosh! Out came a flood of painfully honest remarks starting with, "I don't know, because I can't forgive *myself* for anything?"

"Because I can't be kind to you, because I hate myself? Because I'm so fucking tired of hating myself?"

Wowza. That opened a long, heartfelt discussion about life and the self-hate that he carried. It was by far, the most emotional I'd ever seen Bo—bouncing from angry vents about his past, to his frustration of having to maintain the "macho" fireman identity, to doubts about why he was in a relationship with his new girlfriend, Kristen, when he felt so unsure about himself.

He also said he was buying himself a house and that they had been talking about her moving in with him. He admitted that she makes him happy, but that he was uncertain about how he felt about that kind of commitment. (Trust me, I felt my own triggering happening, *like a high-voltage Taser to the throat,* but I mostly just listened.)

Gritting his teeth, he said, "God, I am so broken right now, and I don't know why or how to fix it."

I empathized with his confusion and told him something that I said to him often, "You're more than a firefighter. You'll figure this out."

He said he was starting therapy soon and thought maybe that would help. I told him that it seemed like he was going through some changes, and that comes with growing pains.

"Why does it have to feel so fucking awful?" he asked me.

"It only feels awful if you resist it," I answered.

"Yes, ma'am," he said, sounding spent.

When I went through the Dark Night of the Ego, I said afterwards, "what needed to break, broke."

Was that what was happening to him?

Was he closing the gap between himself and his soul mothership?

Where was this heading?

A few days later I got a text from him saying,

"I'm sorry. I'm going to cut contact from you for a while because I'm in a relationship.

Kristen and I are moving in together."

fuck

Fuck.
*&%$#&%#x%@!!

Arrrrrrgggghhhhhhhh!

Eat, Pray, Love, Crap.

Geezus, they hardly knew each other! There were red flags all over it! What the hell was he thinking?

I responded to his announcement with a barrage of messages stating those points exactly.

I'd ask him things like ...

Why was he was giving up on his dreams of retiring and having his freedom to do this? Did he just want happy in a relationship or did he want a relationship that challenged and grew him?

To which he wouldn't respond.

Then I asked him ...

If he hates himself, how did he think he was ever going to really love her? And why the rush?

To which he still didn't respond.

Then I told him I thought his decision was needy and immature.

To which he did respond.

He told me he thought I was being mean.

"Mean?! Oh, shut up, you thick-headed dumbass," I said to myself. *"You're just trying to play the victim with me because you know you're being so stupid. I'm just being honest, and you don't like what I'm saying, that's all. You know I'm right and blah ... blahh ... blahhhhhh..."*

I saw it.

I was getting mean.

Fuck. Fuck. Double fuck.

Yes, I was hurting, and maybe he was playing the victim, but that didn't give me the right to question his actions like I was. Even if we were soulmates, we weren't together and we hadn't been for a while. It wasn't my life, it was his. And he was doing what felt comfortable and right to him for his own reasons.

He just wanted to feel good, which is all any of us ever want.

Despite what I'd been hearing from him, he obviously still had an ocean of resistance to awakening. It just was what it was ... and it *wasn't* the dramatic, rejection crisis that Helen was making it out to be.

In a moment of clarity, I saw that my machine gun fire of messages and insults at him was really me avoiding my own deepest emotions.

What those messages were really saying was,

I feel sad and scared right now, and I wish this wasn't happening.

Then I also saw that my feelings are just that, my feelings inside of me, and I needed to deal with them. I was going to have to find some introspection and faith that I was going to be all right.

I sent him a message. I said I was hurting, and that I was sorry for the bullying. "Forgive me," I said.

"Yes, ma'am. Of course. You've forgiven me plenty," he promptly replied.

I was proud that day that I had grown enough to recognize, as Wes likes to call it, my "less skilled" behavior.

Well, dear Bo had helped me close the gap between me and my soul, and he had definitely been the catalyst for my awakening

... but maybe that was all he was ever going to be.

(sigh.)

Fuck.

## chapter eighteen

a bunch of dead guys

As I boarded the groovy, colorfully air-brushed, converted school bus, I said to the driver, "The Muppets called. They want their bus back."

"Tell them they can't have it," he answered back.

The Muppet shuttle was headed to a little mountain town called Nederland. Alex and I were headed to our first "Frozen Dead Guy Days."

Nederland's "Frozen Dead Guy" is a Norwegian grandfather named Bredo. Bredo believed in cryonics, which is the preservation of people through freezing, with the hope that resuscitation and restoration to full health may be possible in the future. Upon his death, about thirty years ago, Bredo was brought to the U.S. by his daughter and grandson to be cryogenically frozen, which he was, in California. The pair then brought him to Nederland where they intended to start their own cryonics facility. Bredo was put in a Tuff Shed and kept on ice while they worked on their venture.

Eventually, however, the grandson was deported for visa reasons, and the daughter was going to be evicted from her home for not meeting water and electrical codes. That's when a local reporter got involved, broke the story to the city of Nederland that Grandpa was being kept in a Tuff Shed, and it became national news. The city of Nederland had to pass a law outlawing the keeping of dead bodies on private property following the news but Bredo was "grandfathered" in under the law and allowed to stay.

He's still there in a Tuff Shed, being kept on ice by a monthly caretaker.

The Frozen Dead Guy Days festival started about fifteen years ago and is music, food, drinking, and weird events like a Grandpa look-alike contest, frozen turkey bowling, and a polar plunge into the local icy lake. Tuff Shed is one of the main sponsors.

As Alex and I walked through the crowd lining the streets for the hearse parade, there were adults, kids, dogs, and crazy costumes everywhere. I even saw a guy in a yellow Teletubby suit.

Alex said he wanted to go find the brain freeze contest.

I told him I was going for a funnel cake, and we agreed to meet later, down at the coffin races.

As I walked the streets of delightful twistedness, I decided the part I like most about Frozen Dead Guy Days is it's accepting attitude about death. I think it's perfectly healthy to have a lighter attitude about something that is natural and inevitable. The mortality rate is 100% after all. Everyone who walks this planet eventually dies, and there's no right or wrong way as to how or when that happens. It just does. Nowhere is it written that we all are entitled to die peacefully at age eighty-five in our beds. That's an ego construct that the universe never agreed to.

Death does not frighten me. To me, it's just our transition from a physical state back to a blissful, non-physical state—where we can still observe, and help guide, all that is physical. It's never a punishment, separation, or tragedy for the one who dies. I'm completely confident that Bredo joyfully watches his own festival every year. Who he truly is, who I am, who we *all* are never stops existing. We just turn in the leases on our human bodies every lifetime (or put them on ice) and naturally and peacefully fully rejoin our souls for a while.

Right around this time I'd discovered a group of dead guys that I had taken great delight in.

Their name is "Abraham."

Wow, how do I begin to explain Abraham?

Let me rip a sheet of aluminum foil while you open your mind, and I'll explain who Esther is first. Esther Hicks is a delightful, intelligent woman from Texas, in her sixties, with an amazing voice, who translates communication from a collective crew of souls called "Abraham." Abraham literally converses through Esther. No shit. (Esther is not the first person who has done this over the years. There are others, as well—like Patsy the psychic—Esther is just currently the most popular, well-known, and respected.)

Esther holds workshops around the world where people can come and ask Abraham questions. There is absolutely no subject off-limits, you can ask anything. They've been doing this for around thirty years. There's hundreds of snippets of those workshop sessions, on all different subjects, on YouTube.

And again, if all this sounds like **seriously weird hippie dippy bullshit** to you (I can see you looking cockeyed right now), hang with me. Frankly, when I first heard about Abraham it freaked me out. I didn't want to listen.

Then I decided I was being a hypocrite, because if I used to read the Bible for years and accept that Source could speak through a burning bush, then why should I not believe, 2,000 years later, that present-day God/the Universe/Steve could communicate through a person as well? It took me a while, but when I felt ready, I listened … and I have never heard such unbelievably brilliant, spot-on teaching in my life.

Abraham speaking through Esther is the most logical, intriguing, enjoyable, and funny (yes, funny!) teaching I have ever heard. Collective divine higher consciousness knows what the hell is up. I seriously love Abraham. Abraham is love.

I found that Abraham's messages funnel down to this:

Satisfaction with our relationships, wealth, health, and happiness is directly related to our "alignment" (connection) with Source energy, aka your soul. Getting into alignment means caring about how you *feel*. It's purposely shushing your ego, calming the mind, and allowing a resistance free, open connection between you and Source. Abraham suggests meditation as the best way to get into alignment. Being in nature also helps.

Just lying in bed and *really* relaxing ("beditating") works pretty well for me.

When I'm in alignment, I feel fearless, satisfied, and optimistic. I focus on myself. I feel like Wonder Woman.

When I'm out of alignment, I feel insecure, needy, and full of worry. I focus on what others think of me. I feel like Helen.

It takes practice, but once you get the feeling of alignment, it gets easier and easier to get there.

Abraham also teaches the Universal Law of Attraction ... that what we consistently focus on is what becomes our life experience.

Our thoughts become things.

Life isn't just happening to us, we're always attracting what's happening around us by our own thoughts and emotions. In the same way that radio waves send vibrations, we humans are always sending out vibrational frequencies with our thoughts and feelings ... which the Law of Attraction then matches up with similar vibrations.

If we consistently focus on and believe a thought, the Law of Attraction will eventually bring it into our life experience, whether that's good or bad. That means the possibilities are endless in any direction.

If on the deepest vibrational level, you truly expect and believe, *"I usually get the outcomes I desire,"* then yes, you'll usually get the outcomes you desire. If you go around thinking (like I do), *"Shit, I'm always late,"* then the Law of Attraction will deliver that expectation as well, and you'll always be late.

I know it's easy to assume that the thought is following the action, but it's the other way around. What's happening is doing so because, at some level, you were believing it *first* and the Law is delivering it.

I believe Jesus was talking about the Law of Attraction when he said, "According to your faith let it be done to you."

The cool part of the Law of Attraction is that with deliberate focus, we can co-create with Source a path to anything we desire. God/the Universe/Steve will send you signs and impulses to act on to get you down the path.

The uncool part about the Law of Attraction is when we keep attracting unwanted things because our dominant thinking is coming from that shadow aspect of our personality. For years, I didn't consciously realize that I was thinking of myself as an insecure relationship partner. It wasn't until I had that epiphany that I was the common denominator in all my relationships, that I finally saw how my own negative beliefs about myself kept manifesting in my life. Hence, sometimes we don't even know what we're thinking until we stand back and look at the big picture of what we keep attracting.

Another tricky part of the Law of Attraction is that when you really desire something, you may unknowingly, be focusing your dominant vibration more on the *lack* of it in your life ... which the Law is responding to, thus keeping that lack there.

It's the difference between negatively thinking and worrying, *"I need more money"* (focusing on the lack), and positively believing, *"My prosperity is coming."*

The Law of Attraction only says "yes," so by being aware of your thoughts, and the positive or negative emotions that you have with them, the potential is there to attract anything and everything you desire.

Getting into alignment is what Abraham calls being "in the Vortex." When I'm in the Vortex, I know everything is always working out for me and all I really need to do is relax more and expect good things to come to me.

In my mind, it's like being in a limitless, tropical hamster ball. In the Vortex, I affirmatively believe, *"I am writing a best seller that will be sold in Target,"* with complete ease of conviction that that reality already exists. (Thanks in advance, Target. You're still my #1.)

Fear doesn't exist in the Vortex, so when Helen clumsily tries to climb into the hamster ball with me, we end up looking like a *The Far Side* cartoon. As soon as Helen tries to get into the Vortex, I am no longer in it and I need to go refocus on alignment.

Life is the optimistic, joyful, fearless experience that it's meant to be when you're in the Vortex. It's a mental state of no resistance. I'd like to live there year round.

What I also learned from Abraham is to appreciate manifesting more, not just manifestation.

We're human beings, so the final product of our wants and desires rarely comes overnight. There's a progression, purpose, and beauty in the manifesting of our desires. Life would be a painfully boring, stale experience if we always jumped to end results and never experienced the process.

My therapist, Wes, and I talked about this one day and he relayed a great example. He said there's an old episode of *The Twilight Zone* where a man dies and thinks he's in Heaven. While he's there, all his wishes come instantly true. He plays a slot machine and wins every time. He's got drinks and women around him in a snap. He thinks this is fantastic at first, but after a short time he finds it brutally unfulfilling and boring.

So, he says to his guide, "If I gotta stay here another day I'm gonna go nuts! I don't think I belong in Heaven. I wanna go to the *other* place."

And the guide says, "Heaven? Whatever gave you the idea you were in Heaven? This *is* the other place."

The anticipation, the creativity, and the challenges to navigate *on the way* to what we want add more value to our life experience than the outcome itself.

When I was working on getting the cartoonist's calendar in grocery stores for that year, I realize now there was much more satisfaction every day in the preparation than in the one day I deposited the big check. Looking back, the journey was the best part.

Focusing on manifesting, not just manifestation, helped me get some perspective on my whole awakening experience. I had spent so much of this experience standing with my hands on my hips, nagging Bo in my mind to, *"Hurry up and awaken already!"* so we can get to the happy damn ending of *Eat, Pray, Love, Crack* that I'd almost forgotten to appreciate all the beauty and growth that was happening in me.

A few years ago, I signed up for a fun run/obstacle course event with a group of women friends. Many of us were in different athletic shape—some more prepared, some less. It was in the ski town of Snowmass Village, which at an elevation of around 8,000 feet, made it an air-gasping kick in the ass. When we signed up, we decided that it didn't matter when anyone finished. We'd all keep it fun and meet at the finish line with no comparison or pressure. That's what I needed to do with Bo. I needed to let him run his course his way, in his time.

And I needed to keep running mine.

And eventually we'd meet at the finish line.

It was time to let go, get into alignment, and start focusing on all the good things happening around me.

Alex and I went to see Green Day in concert during this time, where I learned the hard way that at my age I can't jump to the music without peeing my pants. Something about the music triggered bittersweet sentiment in me. I thought about how this relationship, that started with a simple, sweet inquiry about Hula-Hoop lessons, couldn't possibly have been more unpredictable or life-changing.

As I swayed to the music, I looked up with tears welling, and whispered to Bo's soul ...

"I'll always love you, Babe.

Thank you for everything.

I'll meet you in the Vortex."

## chapter nineteen

you cannot make this shit up

Ok, the synchronicities just kept coming. Round two for the skeptics, who I am now really (really, really) surprised are still reading.

As I kept mastering alignment, I was in the Vortex a lot. And when you're in the Vortex, the presence of Source readily flows through you. I was open to that flow, and God/the Universe/ Steve kept sending me more signs that they were there and that the Law of Attraction is real.

For instance, I started taking some classes at a New Thought Center for Spiritual Living in Denver. "New Thought" fundamentals aren't new at all. Basically, they are that we are one with God and each other (so don't be a dick), that thoughts become things (Law of Attraction), and that there are many great spiritual teachers and theologies in history to learn from.

I was loving the classes, and enjoyed having a group of middle-class, educated, hippie dippy folks to converse with weekly. One day I struck up a conversation with a woman during a break. I told her about this book, and that it is about me finding an unusual soulmate. I told her how it's been a bizarre experience, full of so many unexpected synchronicities, "Like us having the same favorite number," I said.

"That's interesting," she commented, "I have an amazing soulmate husband. We've been married 33 years."

"Ha!" I said. "That's the number!"

"Oh really?" She laughed, adding, "My whole family actually has a favorite number, it's 11."

Really? 11? And 33? In the same brief conversation?

Another happened with Alex as we were on our way to Denver, to see *Kinky Boots*, the touring Broadway musical. On our drive down, we had two unusual conversations in the car. One was about people named Lola (no clue on how that evolved). The other was me telling him about a tearjerking video that I'd just seen. It was about a group of women who had shaved their heads out of loving support for a friend who was going through chemotherapy.

As we sat in our seats at the theater, we watched folks file in.

We both watched as two women came in to find their seats. They were probably in their thirties. One looked very ill and weak. She walked slowly and was wearing a surgical mask and a stocking cap over her bald head.

The other woman was lovingly holding her up and helping her with every step. She looked healthy and fit ... and her head was shaved bald.

It was beautiful. Alex and I just looked at each other and smiled. We were still smiling when the show started ... and revealed that the main character's name was Lola.

I decided to take a trip to Houston to attend an Abraham-Hicks workshop a few weeks later. My departure gate was 33. My return gate was 11.

And then there was this unbelievable story that a friend of mine told me about himself. He was an old friend from high school passing through town to go skiing. We met for lunch one day while I was writing this book. He told me that he had been adopted as an infant and that he had recently found some of his birth family.

What he had also found was that he had a brother, born two years before him, whom his mother had named "Timothy Michael Hamburger" (protecting privacy here). She gave that baby up for adoption, and two years later she had my friend, whom she also named "Timothy Michael Hamburger" and gave up for adoption.

Ok, that alone is weird (and kind of unhealthy, but that's another subject), to have named two children the same name.

But what's even more unbelievable is that my friend was renamed "Paul" by his adoptive family ... and the brother was also renamed "Paul" by his adoptive family. *(jaw-dropping emoji)*

Are you a believer in synchronicities yet? Can these things *really* only be "coincidences"?

I also decided around that time, to see what would happen if I very deliberately utilized the Law of Attraction on the sale of my house. I had been renting out my house in Denver since moving to the sticks, but had recently decided that I wanted to sell it and use the money to keep living my "writer" lifestyle.

As I was working with my Realtor, we decided on an asking price of $350,000. However, in my mind, I knew the market was white hot and decided to set my intention that I would get an offer of $365,000. For weeks, as I was preparing to put it on the market, from the Vortex, I focused and believed, "I will easily get an offer for $365K. $365K. $365K …"

First, I got an offer of $338K.

The second offer was $350K.

Offer #3 (of course) was $365K.

Like I said, you cannot make this shit up.

Carl Jung (who gave us "The Shadow Aspect") also taught us this, "Synchronicity is an ever-present reality for those who have eyes to see."

I undoubtedly had eyes to see

… do you?

## chapter twenty

# of aliens and oil leaks

I wish you could see what I see right now. I'm in Estes Park, Colorado, looking out a window from inside a mountain lodge. I'm at the YMCA Camp of the Rockies; I come up here to write sometimes. It's not an expensive, European-looking lodge, like in the ski towns. It just an old lodge with rustic timbers, high ceilings, a stone fireplace, and taxidermy on the walls.

Through the big window in front of me I see a wraparound porch with rocking chairs. Past the porch is a grassy area the size of a few football fields. In the evening, there will be a herd of elk down there grazing, oblivious to the people around.

Beyond the grassy field are some little cabins that gradually disappear into green, pine-covered hills. Those hills get a little hazier, and lighter in color, the higher up you gaze.

Then at one point in the distance, they stop. And behind them, the massive, snow-covered peaks of Rocky Mountain National Park emerge ... protruding *above* the clouds.

It's unnecessarily beautiful.

It's just showing off.

There's a scene in the movie *Dumb and Dumber* where the good-hearted, dipshit main characters, Lloyd and Harry, think they are driving all night to Aspen. But in the morning, when they don't see any mountains (because they had driven the wrong direction and were now in Nebraska), Jim Carrey's character, Lloyd, comments in confusion,

"That John Denver is full of shit, man."

Let me clarify for those of you who have never been here, that no, John Denver wasn't full of shit. Colorado is extraordinary.

Part of my ongoing awakening experience included travelling to other places where I'd lived in the past. My soul was leading me back to my old digs. I suppose it was part of integrating my old life into my new reality. At first, as I was taking these trips, I wasn't even seeing that that's what I was doing.

I went to Arizona, where I spent some years after college. I went to South Dakota, like I told you earlier, and I thought nothing of it. But when I decided to go to Houston to see an Abraham-Hicks workshop (even though they were coming to Denver a few months later), I wasn't exactly sure why. I felt called to go, assuming it was because there was something in the workshop that I was supposed to hear.

It wasn't until I was in the airport on my way home, cruising a gift shop of Texas merchandise, that it clicked for me that I had also lived in Texas. That's when it hit me, I was going back to old places.

There was one other place that I had been thinking about visiting for months, since my awakening, and that was Las Cruces, New Mexico, where I had spent my college days. I hadn't been back in twenty-five years. As I stood in that Houston airport gift shop, fully receiving clarity from my higher self about my recent travels, I also understood why the night before, I had been talking to two men next to me at a restaurant.

Talk about the Muppets; these two guys were Statler and Waldorf, ribbing each other and making bad jokes. As we talked, the conversation eventually became about how one of them had grown up in, none other than, Las Cruces.

Connecting those two things in my mind is the kind of "impulse" to watch for that I mentioned earlier, when Source is guiding you down a path.

I needed to go to New Mexico.

Alex and I loaded the car and headed south as soon as I got back. I like road trips because careful packing is a non-issue. I brought enough shit for a month. As soon as we crossed the border, I felt like I'd come home again. For the next few days, we went from strolling high-end shops on the plaza in Santa Fe to stopping for gas in dusty little towns with stray dogs wandering about.

I spent a day in Las Cruces being flooded by memories. I explained to Alex, as we passed the football stadium, that our claim to fame in sports was that NMSU had the longest losing streak in the nation—twenty-seven straight games—while I was there. Which, as the fourth-longest losing streak in college football history, is still pretty brag-worthy.

After Las Cruces, we decided to head back home through

Roswell, New Mexico. My God, I thought Wyoming had wide open spaces, there must be millions of acres of undeveloped land in eastern New Mexico. It felt like driving on an empty planet of dirt and shrubs. There was hardly anything on the road to Roswell beyond a few sporadic ranches. I saw one mailbox out there in the middle of nowhere.

All it had on it were four big numbers ... 1111. Boom!

I had always known Roswell had some affiliation with alien lore, but I never knew what the whole story was, and Alex and I were both dying to find out.

Roswell was cool. The streetlights had alien eyes on them, and there were statues of little green men all over town. We went to the Roswell International UFO Museum and Research Center, and my mind is still trying to comprehend what I learned there.

The Roswell mystery wasn't just some hokey myth made up by a few guys in aluminum foil hats (not that there's anything wrong with aluminum headgear).

In a nutshell: In early July 1947, over a period of a few days, people from all over the country were reporting seeing a small cluster of saucer-like discs in the sky, traveling at high speeds. There were newspaper articles from coast to coast about it that week. Nobody knew what they were.

During that time, a rancher near Roswell found some unidentifiable debris in a field. He took it into town, where the investigation of what it was got quickly taken over by the military at the local airfield. The government later declared that the debris was a "weather balloon" and dismissed the whole thing. What I got at the museum, though, was numerous firsthand stories of people from the base and Roswell who were involved in the investigation, who said (some on their deathbed) that it was a crashed alien craft and that at least one alien body was found with it.

I don't know for sure what happened back in Roswell in 1947, but I'm open now to the possibility that it was aliens. It's more insane to me to think we're the *only* intelligent life form in existence than to think we're not. I mean the Hubble telescope tells us there's roughly at least 100 billion galaxies out there. Given the numbers alone, it would be completely illogical to think that we're the only life in existence.

Helen doesn't like aliens because she assumes they would be here to invade and destroy her. Mostly, I suppose, because she always finds those different from her scary, and because it's true, the cows usually get abducted first in the movies. She definitely preferred the weather balloon story.

My higher self and Spock logic, however, say that absolutely life from other planets might want to check out our beauty and mayhem with curiosity, so let's not be dicks about it! Let's put up a welcome banner. That's why Roswell is so cool, they roll with aliens being real.

I'm with them. Screw the weather balloon story.

It was aliens.

As Alex and I headed north out of Roswell, into the other side of the middle of nowhere, my car warning system started chiming madly and blinking, "Oil pressure low. Turn off engine."

Cripes.

I got out and checked the oil. It did seem low, so I added some that I had in the trunk and we continued down the road.

The warning went off again.

What the hell? Was I burning or leaking oil? I didn't want

to blow up the engine by not having enough oil, but in reality, it seemed fine. I was confused.

I decided to keep driving, slowly, with the sensor going off, to the next town.

As I drove, I clenched the steering wheel, with the radio off, listening for the slightest wrong noise under the hood. Alex was in the passenger seat sharing in the nervous silence, huddled under a hooded poncho, looking like E.T.

We made it to the next small town where I stopped at an old, dirty gas station to check the oil again and to pee.

Alex looked out the window and commented, *"This looks like a place where people come to get murdered."*

I laughed at that and out of habit, dug through my purse and started putting lip gloss on in the rearview mirror before I got out.

"*Why* are you primping to use a gas station bathroom?" he asked.

It was a valid question.

I put the lip gloss away, opened my door, and answered,

"Because I want to look *good* when they find my body."

I survived the restroom and checked under the hood again. There was no change and the car was running fine, so we decided to make the second leg of the journey back to Las Vegas, New Mexico, for the night.

And as soon as we hit the road … the warning sensor went off again.

Then it hit me, it's the *sensor* that's on the fritz, not the car.

That had happened before. There was really nothing wrong. When my mind finally accepted that's what was going on, our nervous ride turned back into a nice sunset cruise through northern New Mexico's green ranchland.

I had decided before I left on that trip that I had wanted to start mastering my emotions more. They are the perfect indicators of my alignment with Source, and being more consciously aware of them was the key to maintaining my overall peace and happiness.

As I drove on through the long shadows of late evening that day, I thought about how the car was me and that the warning system was my emotions. I didn't totally ignore the warning, I paid it heed, but after close inspection I could see that there was really nothing wrong. In fact, if I had blindly kept adding oil like the warning system was telling me, I would have ruined the car for no reason.

It would have been the automotive equivalent of self-sabotage.

I was learning to pay much more attention to my emotions and really examine if they were relevant in a situation, or just old egoic dramas from the past getting triggered. Most of the time when it was negative emotions, it was just old drama. I was discovering this in an unusual way.

I started having therapy sessions between my right and left hand.

I had read once that our non-dominant hand is a link to our subconscious mind and ego. So, one day when I was feeling triggered, I wrote with my dominant hand, *"What's bothering you?"* and I was shocked and amazed at how much old pain came through my non-dominant hand writing the response. I had been doing this quirky trick frequently on this trip, and it was really helping me become the neutral observer, and master, of my emotions.

When we got to the hotel later that night, despite everything turning out fine, I was having some feelings of insecurity. So, I sat down for a therapy session with two pens and some paper. What I found was that the car situation that day had triggered feelings of fear and helplessness.

As my left hand sloppily talked it through on paper, my right hand sipped coffee, took notes, and nodded in support. In a short time, it felt resolved, and I felt good again—and that was now my goal—to feel good most of the time and enjoy my life.

Steven Pressfield, in his book *The War of Art,* said this about mastering one's self, "[A]s Socrates demonstrated long ago ... the truly free individual is free only to the extent of his own self-mastery. While those who will not govern themselves are condemned to find masters to govern over them."

I was becoming my own emotional master. I felt like a gangsta.

I guess the perfect lesson, tied to the perfect metaphor that day was this ... the master doesn't just react to the warning system. The master gets out and checks under the hood.

## chapter twenty-one

love is a firehose

I've decided to create relationship kits for all of us.

Your kit contains three things:

1. A brand-new, perfect-condition fire hose

2. Your own fire hydrant, connected to a master, infinite water source

3. A planter box of flowers

The fire hose is your *alignment* to your soul.

The hydrant is your *soul*, connected to Source.

The planter box is your *life*.

Instructions:

Connect your fire hose to your hydrant with care. Once it's properly connected, slowly turn on the tap, and water from your hydrant will start to flow. Use that nice, steady flow to maintain the flowers in your planter box. Take pleasure and pride in your flower box. Make it enjoyable to you and exactly as you want it. It doesn't have to be perfect. Gaze at its colorful blooms, smell the wet dirt, and feel the smooth textures of its leaves every day. Lovingly pull weeds and fertilize when necessary.

Cautions:

-Your hose, flow, and planter are yours and yours alone. You are responsible for their complete care and upkeep.

-You may not ask others to water your flowers if your flow is not working properly. Their water does not work on your flowers, and it depletes the flow to their own (it's a lose-lose).

-Others may not ask you to water their flowers (also a lose-lose).

Manufacturer's advice:

If your flow has stopped, or is insufficient to keep your flowers healthy, we suggest thoroughly inspecting your hose. Look particularly for where your ego is blocking the line, as this is the most common cause of insufficient flow. We also suggest naming your ego to establish a friendlier, working relationship with it when this happens (and it will, frequently).

You may also want to look for vices and addictions pinching the line, as they are usually symptoms of a much larger problem with your flow that will need to be addressed.

Stretching your hose too far or leaving it in a tangled mess may also hinder your flow, so careful inspection and meditation (or beditation) should be done, preferably daily, to maintain a good connection.

We here at "Love Is a Fire Hose, Inc." do understand that

there is a compassionate temptation to want to offer and/or borrow water from others when there are problems with flow. We understand; we're not dicks. But as that will not provide you with the best results possible, we only warranty the flowers being watered by you, with your own equipment, as clearly instructed.

We suggest that when you do observe a neighbor or partner's low flow and/or wilting flowers, it is best to offer encouragement and lovingly suggest they refer to their instruction manual. This approach doesn't deny them the valuable, necessary experience of learning to fix their own connection and flow.

Our kits are created for everyone, and we firmly believe that every person can fix and maintain their own flow with moderate attention. If further instruction is required to unblock one's flow, we suggest pursuing books, videos, or local therapists that resonate with you.

We also understand that at times, you may have an unexpected, freak blockage or hail storm that radically destroys your flowers. These things happen. No worries, you only get one planter box (this time around), but you may continue to plant and re-plant new flowers as desired. Do-overs are allowed.

Maintaining your own fire hose, flow, and flowers is the key to your relationship happiness. Ultimate satisfaction will come in the confidence that you can maintain a brilliant, beautiful flower box all on your own. Plus, we offer a 100% guarantee that others who are maintaining their boxes with the same care and love (or not)—per the Law of Attraction—will soon gravitate to you and you toward them.

So, be the gardener that you want to attract, friends!

* * *

That's what this kit is about. Relationships that start with two equals taking well-maintained responsibility for their own happiness first.

Over a year now into this awakening and healing journey, here's what's in my Vortex now … a loving, soul (or groovy karmic) partnership where we both maintain our own fire hose, hydrant, and flowers every day.

What is not in my Vortex … a partner to legally commit to me *'til death do we part.*

Am I saying traditional marriage is a bad thing? Yes and no—it depends on the intention behind it. If it's a celebration between two happy gardeners in alignment in the Vortex, then marriage can be a wonderful thing. But if it's between two out-of-alignment egos who equate marriage with security, then no, it's not a good thing.

I understand the desire for weddings. I had two of them. They're a fancy public display of love. They're fun and free drinks. But let's be honest, they're about making a life-long commitment that many people can't keep for good, realistic reasons.

I don't think the divorce rate is high because people don't know how to commit. I think it's high because we don't know how to choose good relationships in the first place. Because many of us, like all the sweet June Fucking Cleavers, unknowingly have childhood wounds and unmastered emotions choosing for us.

I also think the divorce rate is high because a life-long commitment to *anything*, often made when we're young, is simply a damn tall order to fill.

Nowadays I prefer the idea of joyfully choosing to love one special person every day, in the present. The only lifetime commitment of love that I truly need already exists, in my connection with my Source.

I have an old friend from childhood who was always an open-minded, carefree soul. When he and his wife got married out in the woods, in a personal (non-legal), spiritual ceremony, other friends later joked that they weren't sure if the couple, proximity-wise, got married "by the trees" or if they were actually "married by the trees." That will never not be funny to me, and now I think my friend and his wife had the right idea.

I think getting married by the trees, in our own personal way, is where it's at. Let's focus on the spiritual, unconditional love factor … and get codependency, government, and insurance out of marriage.

If I ever *did* get married again, I'd make my hippie, non-legal vows something like this,

"I, Julie, promise you, Timothy Michael Hamburger, that I will do my best to keep in alignment with my soul, so that I may offer you the absolute best of my love, my loyalty, and my whole heart for every day of our lives that we are together."

Then he'd say the same, we'd put some rings on it, and the trees would proudly pronounce us "two damn cool people" to the rest of the forest. We'd have a big party afterwards that looked like the end of a *Shrek* movie.

Premarital counseling, facilitated by the trees, would be done as individuals not as a couple, and would include this checklist:

1. Have you learned to separate your ego from your soul?

2. Have you done your shadow work and mastered your

emotions?

3. Do you take full responsibility for your own happiness, thus surrendering all rights to blame the other for *your* feeling insecure, depressed, angry, and/or overall douchey? Check, check, check. Good.

I think that's where we're headed in this world. I know that's where you'll find me. Even people who are already married could mentally back up to being individuals, go through tree-marital (bwahaha) counseling, and get married again. This time, purely spiritual, by the trees. That would be a lovely thing.

Now, some folks may dramatically "gasp!" and clutch their chests at my saying that it's time we evolve out of the old legal model of marriage into a more spiritual model. Those folks may assume that partners will cheat or leave without a legal commitment ... which is revealing a lot about their own subconscious fears (sounds like a session to have with the non-dominant hand to me). I don't agree, because I think that assumption underestimates our natural desire for meaningful relationships. Just because a partner could stray doesn't mean they'll want to. Most people don't want that. A healthy partner on your same vibration will love to stay and tend their garden next to yours. Relax, it will be each other's joy to stay.

Our relationships are evolving because we're all evolving.

It's all good.

So, focus on your own flower box and alignment. Name your ego, do your shadow work, master your emotions, and take responsibility for your own happiness.

And just think how beautiful the world will be when billions of us are watering our flowers, side by side.

chapter twenty-two

***

eat, pray, love, crack

I told you I'd keep writing this memoir of a meat suit until we found out together how *Eat, Pray, Love, Crack* ends.

Spoiler: There is no traditional, wrap-it-up, romantic ending. It's sweeter ...

My soul and I live happily ever, ever, ever, ever, ever after.

And after all you just read, I hope you all can celebrate the sweetness of that, too.

I will probably never fully understand what Bo and I are to each other until I croak and fully rejoin my soul on the mothership. Why *did* all this happen? Was he really the catalyst for my awakening because we're soulmates out of whack? And why is there a worldwide community of other people describing this same experience?

I don't know for sure.

I also don't know when or if he'll awaken and meet me in the Vortex.

What I do know is, I'll love him just the same if he does or doesn't.

When I'm truly in the Vortex, it doesn't matter to me if he's there or not … which I now see was the point of this whole crazy experience. In the Vortex, I know that I am good enough—for me, for him, for anyone to love—even with my swearing and my napkin hoarding. I never needed to become the Buddha or Pollyanna in this. I just needed to unlearn a lot of old, useless beliefs that were holding me back from my own happiness.

Bo was never a jerk for leaving. He left because he was on a very different vibe and because, well, this probably confused the hell out of him given what he believed. If it had been the other way around, I'd likely have left, too.

I mentioned earlier that the final stage of twin flame relationships is union. So, someday, I suppose, we might find each other again, this time in the Vortex. That will have to be the sequel though. Because for now, I think this part of the journey stands on its own and should be shared. The manifesting matters as much as the manifestation, remember?

No matter what happens, my soul ginger will always have permanent real estate in my heart and my deepest appreciation for helping me close the gap between me and my soul in this lifetime.

So, now you know what can happen if you call your own twin flame/perfect storm of dysfunction with a twist into your life.

I know for me, writing about my spiritual awakening experience has been like describing a mango to you. I can describe what a mango looks like—the color, the texture, the shape, etc.—but you can't fully experience a mango unless you taste it. I don't expect you to completely understand my experience (hell, I don't even completely understand my experience) until it happens to you.

Is consciously becoming aware of our egos, and thus awakening to our souls, the next step in mankind's evolution?

You and your ego get to decide that for yourself.

All I know is

1. I couldn't have made this up if I tried.

2. I'm glad God/the Universe/Steve told me to write this down, because if *Eat, Pray, Love, Crack* entertained you and helped you understand your own awakening symptoms (and thus feel a little less like Harry Potter under the stairs), then I've successfully fulfilled my part of this *Star Trek* love mission.

A lot of what I've said here about religion, God as The Force from *Star Wars*, reincarnation, synchronicities, and the Law of Attraction are big paradigm shifts … and those come with resistance.

I know.

Ten years ago, I wouldn't have believed 90% of what I just wrote.

Change of ideas can be uncomfortable (imagine how it felt at the time to accept that the world wasn't flat), that's why our egos mock them and call them things like hippie dippy bullshit. But I can tell you through my experience, the emotional discomfort came only from my resisting the truth that was presenting itself. The mental misery that I felt was solely because Helen was clinging hard to my old beliefs.

If you're being called to a new understanding of your own soul and the universe, as I was, you can't ignore it and you'll suffer like hell trying. You can't stop your own evolution. You can painfully slow it down, but once it's in motion, it's in motion.

And that's a good thing.

It means the scale is tipping from living your life through fear, to living it through divine love, which is what Heaven on earth is.

I don't think everyone goes through awakening the same way, nor does it require another person to be the catalyst. It can look very different than this and many things can be the catalyst. My advice if it happens to you? Surrender to it and be kind to yourself.

This was all much harder than I thought it would be. Going through the Dark Night of the Ego and the shadow work healing cycles was truthfully, mind-numbing, total misery some days (I've often thought that the first thing I'd say to Bo when we meet in the Vortex is, *"Well, that was easy."*). But I'd do it all over again to be where I am today. Because somewhere between those things, expensive shithole motel rooms, drag queens, psychics, frozen dead guys, and aliens, I now understand what life is about.

It's about love.

The real me, the real everyone, is simply unconditional love, and our purpose here is to create experiences that expand our ability to be that love. It is the common bond that humanity shares, no matter what path that takes. Someday we will all understand that, and encourage one another's journey rather than judge each other's path.

We're just not there ... *yet*.

My shift in consciousness didn't eliminate my ego. No, Helen is still around. She's usually out grazing, but still pops up when salespeople talk down to me and on other triggering occasions. I've come a long way, though, since the screeching, flame-bursting, tipped-over train wreck in the parking lot that day. I can usually get her back to pasture quickly.

I'm newly awakened on the inside, but I'm still pretty much the same me on the outside, with the exception of a few more tattoos. I didn't go buy a bunch of crystals, start wearing patchouli, change my name to Mother Luna, or move into a yurt.

Taco Bell, meat, and I made up and see each other regularly again. I still wear cowboy boots and talk to myself in the car. I understand the Law of Attraction and that I have the guidance of infinite love and intelligence with me always. I study many great spiritual teachers because I know the truth of the universe is mine to decide.

I guess I'm the model of a modern-day spiritualist.

I just bought a pickup truck and am thinking about getting a camper. I think I'll spend more time wandering beautiful places between South Dakota, Wyoming, Colorado, and New Mexico, sleeping under the stars, surrounded by my friends the trees, with Alex likely on the roof in a kaftan trying to contact aliens and/or David Bowie.

Out there I'm going to keep deciding for myself what love is, and who I am, from a place of alignment with Source. That's where every answer I'll ever need is. That's where the limitless possibilities of what's next will hatch.

That's where, as Abraham likes to say, *"life gets delicious."*

Live long and prosper, brave warriors of love.

five years later

So what happened after all this, you're wondering? Well, many lovely things. Amazing Alex left the nest and is adulting wonderfully, Patsy the psychic went home to fully rejoin her soul, I finally learned what a chakra is, and *Hippie Dippy Bulls**t* resonated with folks all across the country (even showing up on Target.com—see page 139).

Bo became single again, and we came back together a few more times over the years. And while the soul love was always there, sadly, there was still too much resistance going on for us to create a harmonious, human relationship. Eventually, we both agreed that it was time to say goodbye ... for good.

He's out there somewhere following his dreams, and I'm now living in mi amor, New Mexico, eating green chili like a wimpy gringo, continuing to write, and following mine. Despite the confusing mess that our relationship very often was, he always whole-heartedly supported my writing this book *and* he woke me up, so I don't harbor any resentment towards him. The hardest part to accept was that he didn't have the same experience, and thus didn't get to reap the benefits of awakening—benefits that I got because of him. I think I awoke because I was already in the vicinity of my own soul; I'd been hearing that calling for a few years before we'd found each other. I suspect he didn't wake up because he was too far away to hear his own soul calling.

His gap was just too big to close for now.

That's Ok. He served me (and subsequently, all of you who've just read this) incredibly well, and I'll always love him. I hope you will, too. And we *will* see each other again someday. Soulmates always reunite, if not while they're alive then when they're dead … because we all go to the Vortex when we die.

So, are twin flame relationships a real thing? Absolutely.

Do twins end up together? Sometimes yes.

Obviously, sometimes no.

Can you move on from your twin flame soulmate and love another in a lifetime? Yes. They are the catalyst for an abundant, joyful life … even if it's not spent with them.

Beautiful Bo helped me to close the gap between me and my soul and there is no bigger gift to give another than that.

He didn't come along to make my life easy, he came to set me free.

Mission accomplished.

The author wishes to express much appreciation to Bo and Alex, especially, for allowing me to share this story. And thank you to Eckhart Tolle, Esther Hicks, Jason Mraz, Jesus, David Sedaris, The Buddha, Imagine Dragons, Wayne Dyer, Jim Carrey, Ralph Waldo Emerson, Russell Brand, Oprah, Deepak Chopra, Boy George, Ray Bradbury, Rones, Gen, Joy, Carrie, Polly, and my Hippie Dippy Editor, Bobby Haas, for being a part of this journey.

"If I have seen further, it is by standing upon the shoulders of giants."
—Sir Isaac Newton

Made in United States
North Haven, CT
21 March 2022

17377463R00105